THE LANGUAGE OF LEADERSHIP

Nicer Bark, No Bite

Praise for
The Language of Leadership

"Whether you believe leadership is inherited or learned, you're apt to agree that many people can develop leadership ability with proper training. *The Language of Leadership* by Daniel Matthews provides practicalities and real examples to strengthen anyone's desire to improve their leadership traits. I intend to expose the jewels of this book to my students in the leadership management course at our university."

Dr. Salah Shakir

Dean of Online Admission and University Technology Adjunct Faculty, Midway University

"Clear, concise, and to the point, *The Language of Leadership* is a book worth having in your library, in your backpack, and on your nightstand. Each chapter has a reflection question and a START activity with an application passport that you can use to chart your progress on your leadership journey."

Phil Gerbyshak

Sales Expert Speaker and Trainer, Leader, and Navy Veteran

"Daniel was my first trainer at Toyota and the lessons he taught me gave me the beginnings of a leadership foundation that would help me succeed at Toyota and beyond. Not everyone can have Daniel as their personal leadership trainer, but his newest book — *The Language of Leadership: Nicer Bark, No Bite* — is the next best thing. Daniel not only shares stories from his decades of leadership experience, which make the practical lessons memorable, he provides readers with a simple and effective way to internalize the skills. His dynamic, approachable style, combined with the layered learning process, engages the reader in a learning experience like no other book I've read. I highly recommend it!"

Tracey Richardson
Author of *The Toyota Engagement Equation*; Co-owner, President, and Founder of Teaching Lean Inc.

"I love this book! It is smart, relevant, and authentic. Dan takes us on a step-by-step journey to being a better leader — one who leads with kindness and clarity. There is a meaningful lesson for each day of the month and a practical application for each lesson. I expect *The Language of Leadership* to be used everywhere by leaders and leadership teams who need a guidebook that appeals to all levels of leadership. Thank you, Dan! I will be sharing this book with the leaders in my circle of influence right away!"

Michael Duke
Retention Expert, Keynote Speaker, and Vistage Group Chair

"*The Language of Leadership* by Daniel Matthews is two books in one. First, Daniel uses engaging stories and quotes to inspire you to become a better leader. Then, in workbook style, he gives you useful exercises to guide you on your journey to world-class leadership. This is the book I needed to help my MBA students achieve their leadership potential."

Bobby Ricks
Retired Professor, Midway University

"*The Language of Leadership* by Daniel Matthews is a must-read for leaders desiring fluency in the related languages of respect, trust, collaboration, reciprocation, performance, and the like. Daniel has skillfully synthesized the pursuit of leadership mastery into 31 practical lessons. With each lesson, Daniel shares practical, sensible, and relatable information and stories. He then challenges the reader to reflect and find personal application for the lesson at hand. Finally, he makes a tool available to monitor the reader's progress. Daniel has created more than a book on leadership — he has created a developmental process in which the reader moves purposefully toward a heightened understanding of the language of leadership. I highly recommend this book!"

Phillip Van Hooser, MBA, CSP, CPAE
Author of *Leaders Ought to Know* and *We Need to Talk*

"*The Language of Leadership* by Daniel Mathews is a practical, focused, organized tool for individuals who want to become more effective leaders. As a business strategist and executive coach, I find many managers in my client organizations who are serious about developing their leadership competencies. I am recommending to them that they get a copy of this book, and work through the process outlined at the beginning of the book. Anyone who follows the process and applies the wisdom contained in this book cannot help but become a more effective leader."

Stephen Tweed, CSP
CEO, Leading Home Care; Founder, The Home Care CEO Forum; Author of *Conquering the Crisis: Proven Solutions for Caregiver Recruiting and Retention*

"I wish I'd had this practical leadership book in 1981 when I transitioned from a Territory Manager to a District Manager position, and was expected to know how to lead. Back then, many new salesmen were given the keys to a company car and a map. And new managers were often simply given the keys to the office and introduced to their team. I was fortunate to have excellent leaders and mentors for both positions but *The Language of Leadership* by Daniel Matthews would have been a valuable addition to our professional training library. I believe it would have been our #1 resource to study, apply, and report on at our quarterly review meetings. It would have made our lives easier and more successful. Now that I'm retired, I will still use the principles taught in this book in my daily relationships and as I build my latest venture, a podcast called *Bluegrass Region Voices and Views*."

Tom Hailey
Retired Sales, Marketing, Business Development, and Continuing Education Executive; Creator and Host of "Bluegrass Region Voices and Views"

"Daniel Matthews has truly created a roadmap for becoming a first-time leader or improving leadership skills. With compelling examples and stories, as well as actionable steps designed to reinforce each lesson, this is a great self-study book or serves as an excellent coach/"coachee" playbook. Its practical and tactile language walks the experienced leader (or the soon-to-be leader) through the "not always common sense" approach to leading people. It can be revisited periodically to brush up skills or as a new blueprint for leading a new team. Your leadership journey starts here!"

Tom C. Johnson
Human Resources Expert; Owner, A.O. Consultants, LLC

"In his book, *The Language of Leadership*, Daniel Matthews helps the reader understand and clarify leadership and relationships through his simple yet powerful learning process. Matthews shares a proven formula that is guaranteed to make you a much more successful leader! He breaks down the elements of leadership into a doable, actionable, measurable process through his 'Leadership Education and Application Passport.' On its own, this end-of-each-chapter tool makes this dynamic book worth buying. Don't miss this exciting opportunity to turn the corner on your leadership. Your team will thank you!"

Elizabeth Jeffries, RN, CSP, CPAE
Executive Leadership Coach and Author of *What Exceptional Executives Need to Know*

"Dan and I worked together during the startup of Toyota's first North American manufacturing plant in Georgetown, Kentucky. We were part of a team developing and delivering training to introduce new supervisors to the thinking and skills they'd need as successful leaders in a Toyota operation. One core lesson stressed Toyota's view about the responsibility of the leader: 'If the student hasn't learned, the teacher hasn't taught.' That sentence puts the role of the supervisor front and center; it is your job to make sure your team members have the path, the means, and the skills to succeed. That message comes through in the 31 lessons of Dan's new book, *The Language of Leadership*. What's more, Dan's lessons go beyond just *telling* to truly *reinforcing* in a very practical and important way. The activities that follow each of the book's lessons stress self-reflection in which the reader is urged to compare her or his intentions, behaviors, and aspirations to basic human wisdom of the lessons. In that way, Dan's book does an excellent job of exemplifying one of its main themes — leadership is a helping profession that succeeds by creating the environment and relationships in which others can use their capability to learn, grow, and be effective and successful."

David Verble
Former NA Toyota Manager; Partner at the Lean Transformations Group; Lean Enterprise Institute Faculty

"Finally, a leadership book that offers practical, actionable steps! I loved Daniel Matthews's new book, *The Language of Leadership*. Matthews has given us a course in leadership by offering 31 short but impactful chapters. Each of the lessons can stand alone, allowing the reader to read, reflect, and — most importantly — take action! I can see organizations using this as a mandatory text for everyone in leadership. Highly recommended."

Cathy Fyock
Author, *The Speaker Author: Sell More Books and Book More Speeches*

"Daniel Matthews takes a comprehensive approach to leadership development in *The Language of Leadership*. It is truly a toolkit consisting of lessons, relevant examples, and activities to make the learning applicable. Daniel draws from his depth of experience to bring common, frustrating leadership challenges to life and then offer solutions that uphold dignity and respect for others. In addition to being a quality toolkit, this book is a thoroughly interesting read!"

Lisa Johnson, SHRM-SCP
Owner, HR Know-How, LLC

"There is a humility in this book that is rare and precious, a kind of generosity of spirit we don't often see in business leaders — who tend to be reticent to talk about their own successes and failures despite the universal truth that doing so can help others to learn and be inspired. In *The Language of Leadership*, Daniel Matthews opens his heart (and his humor) and offers up sharp, game-changing insights as he reflects on 31 leadership lessons he has learned – sometimes the hard way – in his career. His stories and suggestions always drive home clear messages and principles so that we, as readers, can be stronger and more impactful in our own efforts to lead, grow and improve our teams. Throughout my career, I've struggled to always bring my best self to leadership moments, offering what Daniel calls a 'nicer bark and no bite,' and this practical, approachable book has helped me tackle the big task of 'being a better leader' by breaking down my efforts into daily lessons and reflections, and follow-up activities that help me apply what I have learned. Daniel Matthews has created a management degree in a book, worthy of reading and re-reading by anyone charged with or called to lead others."

Kate Colbert
Marketing and Communications Consultant, Entrepreneur, and Author of *Think Like a Marketer: How a Shift in Mindset Can Change Everything for Your Business*

"One of the most important and complicated parts of being a leader is stepping from leadership theory to leadership practice without forgetting what your true purpose is. Through his book, *The Language of Leadership: Nicer Bark, No Bite*, my friend Dan Matthews takes us through that journey from theory to practice, and does so in a way that is both simple and strong. Dan's insights about leadership are reinforced through leadership quotes and personal experiences, and readers are invited into a process of reflection and introspection — getting to know our own abilities and opportunities as we guide and inspire our work teams. *The Language of Leadership* is a book that practically contains all the characteristics a leader should consider and hone while shipping off to the way of excellence."

Abel Gomez
Shingo Master Trainer and Certified Shingo Examiner; Executive Director of Opex Academy

"For the past decade, I have personally observed Dan Matthews as a leader, teacher/trainer, and professional speaker. In his new book, *The Language of Leadership*, Dan uses a unique and effective layered-learning approach that bridges the gap between the knowledge component of leadership and the guided experience of applied leadership. Following the plan that Dan lays out will certainly build confidence and shorten the learning curve for those new to leadership; it will likewise refresh and inspire experienced leaders. *The Language of Leadership* supplies the missing elements that nurture leaders to the next level of successful performance in a way that is enjoyable and easy to understand."

Doug Semenick, CSP
Leadership Speaker, Coach, and Consultant

"Leadership comes in many forms, but it doesn't happen over-night. Becoming a leader is a gradual transformation that requires you be dedicated, open and receptive to change, and able to pivot and adapt to any environment. Daniel's book offers an insightful account about the lessons he learned along the way, which made him pivot and realize the right path to becoming an effective leader. If you want to become a better leader and avoid some of the pitfalls, READ THIS BOOK!"

Jeffrey Hayzlett
Primetime TV and Podcast Host, Speaker, Author, and
Part-Time Cowboy

"*The Language of Leadership: Nicer Bark, No Bite* offers the right information at the right time. It lays out a really good way to learn what it means to be or become a better leader. In my work as a manufacturing consultant for a manufacturing extension part-nership (MEP), I am constantly running into companies that need leadership training, which can be anything from helping their new front line leaders understand what they need to know, all the way to middle management who may never have really 'gotten' what it means to be a leader. And while we offer them a variety of training to help improve, they often need much more. We do the best we can but many times the training dies a slow death because the ideas are not passed on and used. But the ideas in Daniel's book clearly spell out a great way for any company to keep passing the training on to others. As Daniel suggests in the book's introduction, choosing a mentor for yourself enables you to get real feedback on how you're doing. And having a plan for how you will practice is what makes it work. Any company that needs to work on leadership training could easily use this book as a guide to help everyone in the company become better leaders."

Bill Nusbaum
Georgia Tech Enterprise Innovation Institute (GaMEP)

"*The Language of Leadership* is a valuable resource for both established and emerging leaders seeking to lead more effectively by learning continuously about how to engage and inspire their team members. Daniel's stories highlight 31 leadership fundamentals derived from his own successes and failures, and they are truly engaging and relatable to readers at all levels. Knowing that learning happens from doing, Daniel provides structure within the book through his START framework for readers to reflect, practice, and discover their best selves. I highly recommend *The Language of Leadership* for everyone who desires to become a better leader!"

Katie Anderson
Leadership Coach, Consultant, and Author of *Learning to Lead, Leading to Learn: Lessons from Toyota Leader Isao Yoshino on a Lifetime of Continuous L*earning

"Whether you are a seasoned leader or new to leadership, you'll find that this book is absolutely worth your time. *The Language of Leadership* is an exceptional resource for three critical reasons. Number one, Dan has 'been there and done it!' Dan's proven lessons come from his own leadership experience in a range of environments. Secondly, his insights are refreshing and not the same old story or message. And most importantly, the entire book is written to ensure you actually put the lessons into action so you can grow yourself and those you support. This book will serve you well and, more importantly, it will equip you to serve at a higher level in this world of uncertainty."

Manley Feinberg, II
Keynote Speaker, Author, and Business Leader

"Dan's simple, yet elegant, approach to explaining and teaching true leadership values and skills will help thousands of present and future leaders reach their maximum potential. As Dan explains, leadership is not about criticizing others but about showing support, encouragement, and leading by example. History can teach us many valuable lessons and Dan's storytelling ability helps each chapter drive home a valuable lesson or opportunity to look at something from an angle that we may not have thought of on our own."

Curt Jones
Founder, Dippin' Dots and 40 Below Joe

THE LANGUAGE OF LEADERSHIP

Nicer Bark, No Bite

31 CRITICAL LESSONS
TO LEAD, GROW AND IMPROVE YOUR TEAM

DANIEL D. MATTHEWS

SILVER TREE
PUBLISHING

The Language of Leadership: Nicer Bark, No Bite

By Daniel D. Matthews

Copyright 2020 by Daniel D. Matthews

Published by Silver Tree Publishing, a division of
Silver Tree Communications, LLC (Kenosha, WI).
www.SilverTreePublishing.com

Stories shared in this book are recounted to the best of the author's
recollection. Some names have been changed.

Editing by:
Kate Colbert

Cover design and typesetting by:
Courtney Hudson

First edition, August 2020

ISBN: 978-1-948238-29-8

Library of Congress Control Number: 2020915564

Created in the United States of America

Dedication

This leadership book is dedicated to MSGT Ronald L. Thomsen, who was my flight Sergeant when I was stationed at Minot Air Force Base. His ability to see potential inside of me set into motion a life and career without which this book would not be possible.

Contents

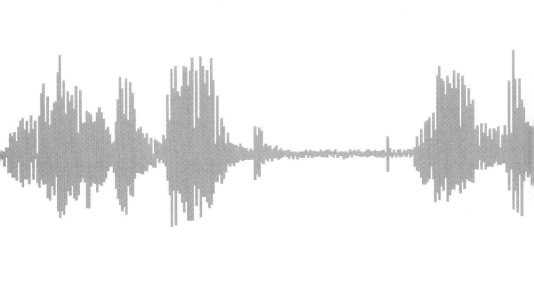

Foreword

By Todd Cohen, CSP

In a world where there is no shortage of leadership books, it's conspicuous that many of those books say much of the same thing — and then stop abruptly at a point of teaching the reader *how to apply the concepts*. In this case, Dan Matthews's new book credibly sets the bar higher. For those of us needing it, this practical, useful leadership book has been a long time coming.

I, for one, struggled earlier in my career, trying to understanding how to be a better leader. I had more than enough theory and concepts, but too few application opportunities. Just because someone was attempting to teach me leadership or what it means to *be* a leader (through a book or through a training program or through direct on-the-job mentorship) didn't mean the concepts were identifiable or relatable to me. In other words, I had to conform to the author, trainer, or mentor's view of leadership rather than developing my own. I was frustrated with people *telling* me how to be a leader and not *showing* me how to find my own leadership style.

Leadership today is no longer about drilling someone in concepts, but rather is about encouraging people to identify and unleash a new mindset and behaviors previously not developed. Leadership can be an elusive skill set that is rarely taught well enough and is often conveyed with a very narrow view and voice. Leadership explained without the crucial *how* is just another fanciful academic exercise lacking in real-world validation. In those cases, it's frustrating that people who have the aptitude to be great leaders don't have the path to make it happen. *The Language of Leadership: Nicer Bark, No Bite* by Daniel Matthews provides that path.

Leadership today is no longer about drilling someone in concepts, but rather is about encouraging people to identify and unleash a new mindset and behaviors previously not developed.

As anyone who has been in the position to teach and develop people can tell you, stories — anecdotal, actual experiences — are a vital part of conveying a lesson and helping people to identify with new concepts, ideas and perspectives. Stories make new topics and concepts immediately understandable and help to remove barriers to deeper comprehension. In this engaging book for leaders at all levels, Matthews has used so many skills from his background to great benefit (like his talent for storytelling), and I found myself eagerly looking forward to each next lesson.

Leadership, how to be a leader, and leading is hard. No one ever said it's a walk in the park. Accordingly, research into leadership (i.e., reading about and studying leadership) is not, in and of itself, good enough to produce leaders. To lead, *one must have led* and then have the chance to translate that leadership experience into success and failures with honesty, vulnerability, and sincerity. So, for a leadership book to rise to the level of practicality and impact, it must first invite readers to apply its lessons to actual, real-time leading at work. The book must also be digestible and applicable to the person reading it. And it must speak across industries and personal backgrounds. On all counts, *The Language of Leadership* exceeds expectations. Dan does an excellent job demonstrating that sound and progressive leadership skills are in the grasp of anyone who wishes to "up their game" and career — if they will commit to learning, reflecting, planning, and applying new methods and skills with their teams. His book helps them do this, through its daily lessons and long-term approach to application. Indeed, Dan has found a way to speak to those of us who want to be better leaders and he shows us a way to make that happen.

As I sit here and write this foreword, we are in the middle of a global pandemic, which makes this book — which is universal and timeless — all the more powerful and timely. The coronavirus outbreak has had distinct impact on businesses and teams, stress-testing people's leadership skills every day in ways previously unimaginable. We need all the help we can get right now, and Dan's examples, stories and lessons give the reader a path of understanding when it comes to *how* to be a good and effective leader, and how to adopt skills that will endure. *The Language of Leadership* delivers its insights with a predictable and impactful cadence: concept, exercise and validation. Simple and powerfully effective is the *how* of this book, and that's what matters. The pandemic will end. Dan's lessons will live on.

I hope you will enjoy this fresh wind of leadership perspective and passion as much as I did.

Todd Cohen, CSP
Keynote Speaker, Sales Motivator, and Author of *Everyone's in Sales: How to Unleash the Power of Sales Culture to Boost Your Revenues, Profits and Growth*

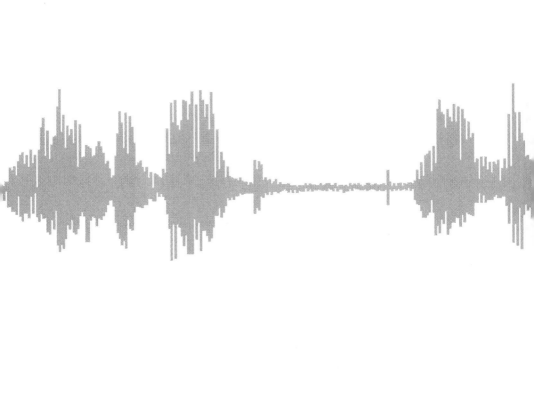

Introduction

"If you don't change, I'm going to have to let you go."

Those words struck fear in my heart. I was a high-school dropout, recently separated from the Air Force, and I was teaching alongside colleagues who had degrees a-plenty: bachelor's degrees, master's degrees, even PhDs. I was terrified that this dream would soon end. Working as a curriculum developer and trainer at Toyota Motor Manufacturing Kentucky was a long way from security guard, construction laborer, carwash attendant, or any number of other jobs that I envisioned for my future when I was growing up. But here I was, enjoying this exciting and important job at a company known around the world as a great place to work.

I was terrified that this dream would soon end.

It was the summer of 1988 when my boss, Jim, sat me down in the first-floor hallway, at the table next to the vending machines, and struck up what was ultimately a very short conversation. He said, "Dan, I've received complaints that you are rude and curt with your students. If you don't change, I'm going to have to let you go. So, fix it or you're gone."

That was the entire conversation. I remember feeling like I'd been hit in the face with a sack full of bricks. Up until that point, I thought

I was doing a great job. Those 31 words motivated me to make a change — not because Jim was a dynamic leader who I didn't want to let down, but because I wasn't ready for the dream to end. But to make a change, I first needed to understand what I was doing wrong. Figuring out what Jim meant by "rude and curt" would be one of the most difficult parts of my transformation. It wasn't until I asked one of my fellow trainers for their insights that I discovered how my words and actions could be construed as negative or even dismissive. I truly had had no clue.

Susan Law and I had been paired with each other to co-teach during our initial evaluation period and had remained confidants. She said, "It's what you say and how you say it. When you're correcting people's answers, you're very blunt. You can sound like a drill sergeant barking out orders. I don't think you are *trying* to be rude or curt; I just think you haven't lost your military edge." I kept listening. She went on, "Your heart is in the right place — you want them to learn and grow. You just need to learn how to bark less like a drill sergeant and talk more like a coach."

Learning to have a nicer bark and no bite was the first of many lessons I've learned during the past 30+ years. And I'm still learning.

Learning to have a nicer bark and no bite was the first of many lessons I've learned during the past 30+ years. And I'm still learning.

Making a Commitment to Nurture and Develop Your People

If you want to be a leader who gets results (and I'm guessing you are, because you're reading this book!), you have to be committed to nurturing and developing your team members so they not only survive but *thrive* in your organization. Their experience depends a great deal upon you. You can't just hire them and set them loose, as much as you might wish you could. I've seen too many examples of leaders who hire an employee to fill an open position and then forget about them ... until they do something wrong. This "hire and forget" style of leadership will cost your company tens of thousands of dollars each year in turnover alone. When someone accepts a job as a leader — overseeing big projects, lots of employees and contractors, and with profit-and-loss (P&L) responsibility — they are often initially motivated by money, power, prestige ... or all of the above. Most will turn out to be average leaders and their team members will have moderate success in spite of the leadership mediocrity that set the tone for their day-to-day work.

The best leaders — those who go far beyond the status quo of mediocrity — focus their time and energy on helping their team members become more successful, by developing relationships, providing feedback and coaching, and by giving them the tools they need to succeed in their jobs.

I am a lucky man indeed to have witnessed and benefited from great leadership in my career. I've seen a lot and experienced the universal highs and lows of career progression, but in unique situations you might find instructive. So here I am, stepping out of the training room and off the conference stage, to share those stories with you. I hope you will find them helpful and inspiring.

Since the beginning of time, we've told stories to share information, to relay our history, and to teach important lessons. Stories fuel our understanding (and retention) of all types of learning objectives. There are many ways to describe my professional path — I've been an Airman (where I led security police and armed-response fire teams), I've been a corporate trainer, I've been a manufacturing-sector HR leader, and I've been a lean consultant, business author, and speaker. And because of all I've seen and done, I've become a passionate storyteller — always looking for stories that I can use to convey lessons I've learned over the years.

This book started with a story about 31 words that made my blood run cold and ignited a fire in me regarding my own self-improvement. Now, based upon pivotal and relatable experiences in my own life, I give you 31 critical leadership lessons every leader needs to lead, grow, and improve.

I learned a long time ago that leaders get work done through people. If you love helping people grow and develop, this book is for you.

I learned a long time ago that leaders get work done through people. If you love helping people grow and develop, this book is for you.

How to Use This Book

Before you dive into the pages that follow, let me give you an idea of what this book will deliver and how to approach the lessons that await you. To help you avoid the scrap training conundrum,[1] this book contains 31 chapters with actionable tools and strategies you can use to lead with a "Nicer Bark, No Bite" — so you can get the results you need.

Each chapter is designed as a stand-alone learning experience. My goal is to provide you with more than just useful leadership tools and strategies; I want to give you the opportunity to apply the learning

---

1   Scrap training happens all too often. It's when an organization sends someone to a conference or workshop at great expense and gets no ROI.

immediately to your real work situations. To that end, here's the best way to use this book.

Think of this book as three trips to the buffet, with some time to let the nourishment settle before you go back for seconds (and then dessert!). This is a book to be marked up, dog eared, and kept at hand for several months (or even forever — it's a great desk reference!).

Step 1: Read One Chapter a Day

First, don't sit down with a whole bottle of wine and read this book in one sitting; take your time. Read one chapter per day for the next 31 days ... before work. You might be thinking, "What difference does it make when I read it? Before work, on my lunch break, or after quitting time?" Because I want you to retain and use what you learn in this book, when and how you read it matters. Your brain deserves time to truly process the lessons that await you. If you read each chapter (I call them "Lessons") before work, one day at a time, the content will be fresh in your mind and your subconscious will start making connections between what you just read and what you're experiencing at work.

Step 2: Take Time to Reflect

Once you've read a chapter and your subconscious has had some time to process it, answer the reflection question at the end of that chapter. Many readers will do this a day or two after reading it. Some will do it the same day, on their lunch or dinner break. The idea is to scribble (in the book or in your own notebook) some detailed thoughts in reaction to the one simple question awaiting you at the end of each lesson.

Step 3: Re-Read the Entire Book (in Whatever Order You Like) and Apply the START Formula

This book is full of helpful acronyms — I'm hoping you like them as much as I do. The third big step in reading and applying this book will happen for you after a month has passed. At the end of the 31 days (i.e., after you have read all 31 lessons), select a chapter (any chapter!) to reread. Then review the answer you wrote to the reflection question for that chapter and apply what I call the START formula. START stands for:

Skill | Target Outcome | Actions | Results | Takeaways

After the reflection sections (which you will have already filled out) will be questions that help you apply the START formula as it relates to the topic of each lesson. Sometimes you can answer these questions in the book itself and other times, you'll want to take out a notebook or a blank sheet of paper. Remember that the best way to use this book is to *use* it, so I encourage you to highlight it, underline it, and write in it.

To take your learning further, and to help ensure you're fully committed and able to apply your new ideas and skills at work, consider enlisting a leadership mentor to participate with you, reviewing your work in the LEAP (Leadership Education and Application Passport) portions of the START activities. A leadership mentor might be your actual boss or another leader you trust (at your company or in an entirely different organization); it could be a peer you admire or a friend who is good at holding you accountable. This relationship doesn't have to be formal or scary — just find someone who is willing to spend 15 minutes with you on each lesson. If you have a spouse who is a savvy leader too, he or she might be a great leadership mentor!

The Leadership Education and Application Passport includes a few fill-in-the-blank exercises and questions, and a place for your leadership mentor to initial the page to celebrate your completion. Think of each passport section as helping you travel to new and wonderful places in the world of leadership.

> If you don't have a leadership mentor, that's a-okay. The learning experience can be richer when you have someone to bounce your ideas off of before you apply your new skills, and it's always nice to have someone with whom you can share your results and takeaways — so they can help you see things you may have missed. But you should read, reflect and apply the lessons in this book in whatever way works best for you!

Repeat the process (read, reflect, re-read, and apply the START formula, and complete the Leadership Education and Application Passport) for every chapter/lesson in the book — all 31 of them! You can choose your own path in terms of which chapters you tackle when. As long as you've read, reflected, reread, and applied the tools and strategies from each of the 31 chapters, you'll be on your way to having developed your own leadership style, which you can activate in your own way and on your own terms.

Fast-Track Your Leadership Acumen

I can tell you that I wasn't a great leader when I first started my leadership career in the Air Force. I'm not even a great leader now. But I am the best *kind* of leader — the same kind of leader you can be: a learning leader. I wrote this book to help you shorten your leadership learning curve, though I hope you'll keep learning always.

My hope is that you take the content of this book to heart so you can become the leader you've always dreamed of being: Achieve more, progress faster, and find workplace satisfaction. I believe you have what it takes to step up, stand out, and inspire others — to create a remarkable career for yourself and a healthy, happy, productive work environment for your teams.

Let's get started!

Progress Scorecard

Leadership can't be learned just through reading. It must be experienced. This book is designed to allow you to *experience* each of the 31 lessons in a layered three-phase approach (or four phases, if you choose to enlist a leadership mentor too).

Use the following pages to track your progress by shading in the stars as you go. It will help you remember which lessons you've completed, which ones you have left to choose from, and how much you've accomplished already. Think of it as a scorecard or report card, where you can "check off" your three-part assignment (read it, reflect on it, and start it) for each leadership lesson.

	Read It	Reflect on It	START It
Lesson 1: So, You Think You're a Leader – Finding and Focusing on Your "Leadership Why"	☆	☆	☆
Lesson 2: If They Ooze, You Lose – Building Remarkable Team-Member Relationships	☆	☆	☆
Lesson 3: Let Go of the Leash – Developing Trust in Your Team	☆	☆	☆

	Read It	Reflect on It	START It
Lesson 4: SWITCH Gears – Avoiding Blame and Defensiveness	☆	☆	☆
Lesson 5: It's Not Just About Your Kite – Making Productive Requests	☆	☆	☆
Lesson 6: Avoiding the Garland Effect – Providing Training That Develops Confidence and Competence	☆	☆	☆
Lesson 7: Seeing with Four Sights, Not Four Eyes – Embracing Four Problem-Solving Types	☆	☆	☆
Lesson 8: Performance Before Pedigree – Selecting the Right Players	☆	☆	☆
Lesson 9: You Have My Word! – Keeping Your Commitments	☆	☆	☆
Lesson 10: You're Fired – Making Decisions with Your Circle of Impact in Mind	☆	☆	☆
Lesson 11: Makin' Bacon – Understanding the Difference Between Pet Peeves and Performance Issues	☆	☆	☆
Lesson 12: Kids and Convicts – Developing Your Team's Creative Muscles	☆	☆	☆
Lesson 13: Just One More Thing – Learning to Teach Rather Than Tell	☆	☆	☆

	Read It	Reflect on It	START It
Lesson 14: Leave Your Business Cards Behind – Creating a Development Playbook	☆	☆	☆
Lesson 15: Painting a Perfect Picture – Mastering Delegation	☆	☆	☆
Lesson 16: Make It Smaller – Redefining "Listening"	☆	☆	☆
Lesson 17: Feed Your Brain – Expanding Your Creativity	☆	☆	☆
Lesson 18: Stop, Drop, and Roll – Maintaining Professionalism Under Pressure	☆	☆	☆
Lesson 19: Get 'er Done – Creating a Culture of Accountability	☆	☆	☆
Lesson 20: Does Your Coffee Taste Like Tea? – Establishing Strong Standards	☆	☆	☆
Lesson 21: That's Stupid – Responding to Bad Ideas	☆	☆	☆
Lesson 22: One Size Does Not Fit All – Delivering Effective Feedback	☆	☆	☆
Lesson 23: The Daily News – Taking the Company's Emotional Temperature	☆	☆	☆

	Read It	Reflect on It	START It
Lesson 24: No Good Deed Goes Unpunished – Learning to Use — Not Abuse — Strengths	☆	☆	☆
Lesson 25: The Goldfish Principle –Laying the Foundation for Success	☆	☆	☆
Lesson 26: One Thing, Just One Thing – Developing an Attitude of Gratitude	☆	☆	☆
Lesson 27: G-Force – Getting People to Gravitate Toward You	☆	☆	☆
Lesson 28: FACE It – Fast-Forwarding Through the Change Curve	☆	☆	☆
Lesson 29: Row, Row, Row Your Boat – Keeping Your Project on Course	☆	☆	☆
Lesson 30: The Bus Lady – Leadership Lessons That Linger	☆	☆	☆
Lesson 31: Free Crab Tomorrow – Stop Procrastinating	☆	☆	☆

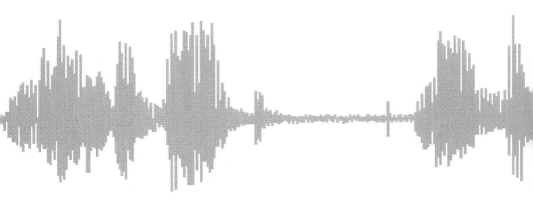

"Great leaders don't set out to be a leader. They set
out to make a difference. It is never about the role —
always about the goal."

— *Lisa Haisha*

So, You Think You're a Leader

Finding and Focusing on Your "Leadership Why"

Think about it for a moment. Leadership sounds prestigious, but it's hard work and comes with great responsibility. In Stan Lee's iconic *Spider-Man* comic books, Peter Parker's uncle tells him: "With great power comes great responsibility." Peter later recounts those words and adds: "This is my gift, my curse." Power, responsibility, gift, and curse all rolled up into one complicated opportunity, leadership requires self-awareness, clarity, and a variety of skills. I believe leadership is a journey worth taking, but one that requires learning, reflection, and repeated application of new skills.

If you ask most leaders, "Would you like to know how to be a better leader?" most will say *yes*! The better question to ask yourself, though, is, "*Why* do I want to be a leader?" If you're doing it for the wrong reasons, you'll never inspire your people to engage and act in the best interests of the organization.

The gift of leadership is the ability to influence your team members by nurturing, caring for, and watching them as they grow and thrive. The curse is the temptation to use your leadership for personal gain rather than good. And like Spider-Man, most new leaders initially take on the role for personal gain: more money, power, control, influence, and status.

The gift of leadership is the ability to influence your team members by nurturing, caring for, and watching them as they grow and thrive. The curse is the temptation to use your leadership for personal gain rather than good.

There is nothing wrong with personal gain or comfort. We all need to do what is best for us and our families, and we deserve a certain amount of reward for our hard work. But once you cross that line into leadership (in business, in non-profit organizations, in communities, or in civil service and politics), your responsibilities go beyond just you and your family, and you find yourself with distinct and implied responsibility to your team members (and *their* families).

Indeed, with leadership comes great responsibility because leaders represent the entire organization. It's been said that "people don't quit jobs — they quit leaders," an implication that people might take a new job because the organization has an inspiring mission, because the work itself aligns with their talents, and because the salary and benefits are attractive. But all those perks can fall short if the leader you report to makes your work days miserable; suddenly, the great company you just joined is an awful leader you're ready to quit. And often, those awful leaders were promoted to positions after performing well in more tactical or executional roles, but were never trained to lead. Now that *you're* a leader (or are aspiring to be one), it's time for you to become the leader your team deserves.

If you want to thrive as a leader, you need to find your "leadership why." The United States Marine Corps has long been heralded for its unwavering values, and its overarching commitment to serve "God, Country, and Corps." In the civilian world, we too should have mottos and unwavering values and areas of focus. The leader's motto should be "service to company, team, and me" ("me" as in you, the reader/leader). To be able to adequately serve your company or organization and your direct team, you must define (and continually hone) who you are as a leader — not just as a contributor to the company, but to your team and to yourself.

Whatever your reason is for accepting a leadership position, you need to know that your boss's expectations and standards of behavior for you are much higher than that of your team members. I know that sounds like an obvious statement, but you wouldn't believe how many leaders go through the day with a status quo mindset until their boss holds their feet to the fire for not meeting a goal or objective. Leadership is not a title or a paycheck or a corner office; it's a set of expectations you must meet. Being ready starts with understanding why you said yes to a leadership opportunity in the first place.

Leadership is not a title or a paycheck or a corner office; it's a set of expectations you must meet.

You need to commit to the company by knowing, understanding, and communicating the mission, vision, and goals in a way that engages your team. You can't just "lip it" — you must live it.

If you're already a leader, you know it takes a lot more than just leading your team. You have to coordinate, motivate, delegate, and organize tasks, reports, meetings, and a host of other activities.

A leader who is committed to his or her team provides a supportive environment, encourages initiative, and makes sure their people have the proper tools, training, and resources to do their jobs. Strong leaders provide coaching, feedback, and opportunities to grow and thrive beyond the team — even helping their people seek and embrace new roles on other teams or even outside the organization, if that's what's in the best interests of the team member's career.

Leadership is demanding, to say the least. Mr. Mizuno, my Japanese coordinator from my days at Toyota, used to say, "Nana korobi, ya oki," a famous Japanese proverb that translates to, "Fall down seven times, get up eight." Failures and setbacks are an inevitable part of the leadership journey. It's those failures that give you the clues you need to move forward. I teach all my clients to think of failure not as a word but an acronym that stands for:

Finding | Answers | In | Life | Using | Reflective | Evaluation

The only way to get up that eighth time is to reflect and evaluate what went wrong the first seven times you fell down. *Fall down seven times, get up eight.*

Leaders don't know what they don't know ... until they dig in and do the work. The more you do, the more you will gain an understanding of what it takes to be a great leader. There will be times when you want to throw in the towel. What you have to keep in mind is your own individual "WHY" for becoming a leader. If your purpose is admirable and ambitious, your path can be rewarding.

Frederick Nietzsche said, "He who has a *why* to live can bear almost any *how*." Here is my twist on his words: "Those who have a *why* to lead can bear almost any *responsibility* or *challenge*."

Knowing why you want to be a leader is the first step to becoming a great leader. Only when you know your leadership "WHY" will you find the courage to stay motivated and to guide your team to achieve new and more challenging goals.

Knowing why you want to be a leader is the first step to becoming a great leader.

Before you walk into work or tuck yourself in for the night, give your subconscious brain something to gnaw on by shifting into FAILURE mode — **F**inding **A**wareness **I**n **L**eadership **U**sing **R**eflective **E**valuation.

Reflection Question for Lesson 1: What difference are you making as a leader?

_____

_____

_____

_____

_____

Time for a break! When you're ready, move ahead to another chapter/lesson and then come back to the following START Activity and Passport exercise during your second read-through of the book.

START Activity

Find and focus on your "leadership why."

START activities should be completed during a second read-through of the lesson, just prior to engaging a leadership mentor or trusted friend to help you with the Leadership Education & Application Passport.

1. Write the following question at the top center of a clean sheet of paper — "Why do I want to be a leader?"

2. Below the question, draw a vertical line down the center of the page.

3. On the left side, write "ME." On the right side, write "MY TEAM."

4. Start with the "ME" side and list all the reasons why moving into leadership would be (or is) good for you.

5. Then, on the "TEAM" side, write down all the reasons why you would be (or are) a good leader for your team. Photograph and scan this list so you can keep it with you wherever you go.

6. Leadership can be tough on you and your family. So, before you walk out the door each day to go to work, read the left side of the list to remind yourself why you are doing it — what's in it for you and what drives you.

7. Before you walk into work each day, read the right side of the list to remind yourself of your responsibility to your team and the company.

Leadership Education & Application Passport

Part A – *Work with your leadership mentor or trusted friend to complete the Target Outcome and Actions section.*

Skill: Finding and Focusing on Your "Leadership Why"

Target Outcome: With whom will you be applying this skill (i.e., your ability to align your workplace priorities and behaviors with your "leadership why"), and what are you hoping to accomplish by doing so?

_____

_____

_____

Actions: What actions need to be taken before and during the application of this skill?

- _____

- _____

- _____

- _____

- _____

Part B – *Now, take a moment to review the results and what you took away from this experience with your leadership mentor to look for ways to improve your next experience using this skill.*

Results:

- _____
- _____
- _____
- _____
- _____

Takeaways:

- _____
- _____
- _____
- _____
- _____

Once you have completed Parts A and B above, have your leadership mentor initial and date the stamp for this Lesson.

Congratulations! You're one step closer to being the leader you've always dreamed of being.

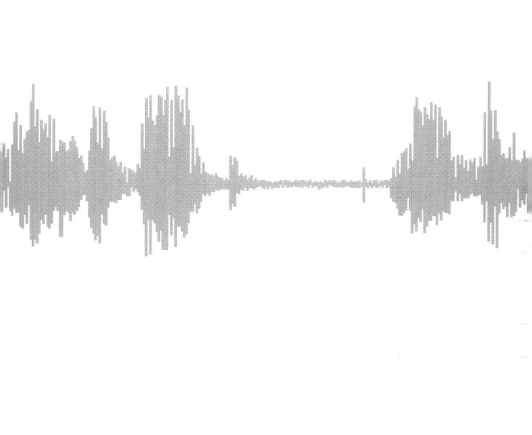

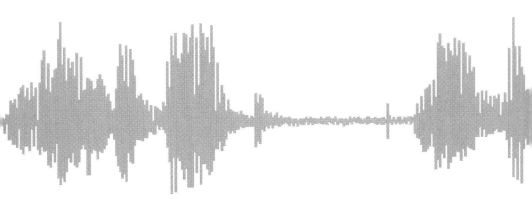

"The fields of industry are strewn with the bones of those organizations whose leadership became infested with dry rot, who believed in taking instead of giving … who didn't realize that the only assets that could not be replaced easily were the human ones."

— *Le Roy H. Kurtz*

If They Ooze, You Lose

Building Remarkable Team-Member Relationships

Imagine reaching into your cupboard for a can and coming out with a hand full of sticky, gooey ooze. That's exactly what happened when my wife reached into our cabinet to grab a can of sliced peaches. The metal can had exploded sometime before, creating quite the mess in the cabinet and, eventually, on her hand. She looked for an expiration date on the peaches, but couldn't find one. This nonperishable disaster left us stumped.

Ask yourself: When was the last time you checked the dates on your canned fruits, vegetables and soups? If you're like most people, you don't. And even if you are the kind of domestic god or goddess who diligently keeps track of food freshness in the pantry or cupboard, you could attest to the reality that most processed and canned goods are stamped with a "Best By" or "Sell By" date — not an "Expiration"

date. So, how are you supposed to tell when a can is getting ready
to explode?

My wife and I took all the cans out of the cupboard and inspected
each one. We found that most of the cans had lids that were bowed
in — slightly indented with circular grooves. This is an indication that
the can is properly sealed and presumably safe to eat. The lids on
three of the cans, however, were bowed out, a sign that the contents
were under unusual pressure (perhaps from bacteria fermenting)
and a good indication that these cans may be the next ones set
to explode.

I'd challenge you to think about employee relationships the way
I now think about canned goods in my cupboard — it's important
to remember that "checking in" on the health or expiration date of
employee relationships is a good way to prevent a different kind of
disastrous "ooze."

Like cans, our team members can find themselves under enormous
pressure and stress. If left unchecked, this pressure can explode
— leaving you (and anyone around you) with a proverbial face
full of ooze.

Picture this ... You are in the lobby of a large company when the
receptionist "explodes." She sweeps all the papers from her desk onto
the floor, starts yelling, and storms outside to smoke a cigarette. She,
my friends, is anything but a "peach" in this moment.

When she comes back in, she's still seething. She says to the visitors
in the lobby, who are watching her with curiosity and wondering if
they should help pick up all the papers on the floor:

> "I'm sick of this! I feel so left out. My leader never includes me in
> the team meetings and she never updates me afterward. I have
> no idea what's going on around here. I'm out here in the lobby

all day — every day — taking care of the needs of our visitors, but nobody takes care of *my* needs."

With that, she grabs her purse and walks out of the building and drives off.

It seems no one had been checking on her expiration date, ensuring she was safe and well-informed and fully engaged in her work and with her co-workers. She oozed, and if her leader isn't thoughtful about how she handles it (and a little bit lucky too), the leader and the company will lose — either through attrition of this valuable employee or because she'll keep collecting a paycheck without delivering her best because she's fed up.

Studies have shown that happy employees are up to 20% more productive than their unhappy counterparts.[1] To be more productive, we need to feel like we matter to the people around us. Humans are social creatures — we crave friendship and positive interactions, almost as much as we crave food and water. So, it makes sense that the better our workplace relationships are, the happier and more productive we'll be.

To be more productive, we need to feel like we matter to the people around us.

Let me ask you this: How will you know when your direct reports' lids are beginning to bow out?

The secret is to check in frequently. It's simple, really; like cans, people should be "checked" on a regular basis. For cans (not that

---

1   Oswald, Andrew J., Proto, Eugenio and Sgroi, Daniel. (2015) "Happiness and Productivity." *Journal of Labor Economics*, 33 (4). pp. 789-822.

I'm an expert), I'd suggest every three to six months. For people, check every day.

To keep the lid on, act like a VIP, which is an acronym you can use to remind yourself about the importance of proactively improving your worker relations. Here's what it looks like to treat your team members like VIPs:

- First, be **VISIBLE**. Make sure they see you every day. Even if you are out of the office, you need to be visible. Send an email or text. Better yet, send a video email or chat via Zoom, even if only for a couple of minutes. Being available to them lets them know they are visible to you. You *see* them and you care about them.

- Second, **INTERACT** with them. Say good morning and make sure you include their name. Our name is our identity. Without a name, good morning is just a meaningless gesture.

- Third, **PROBE**. If you want to build good working relation- ships, you need to make your interactions with your team members about *them*. To learn more about your team members, ask questions without being intrusive. Find out what's going well, what's not, and how you can help. Inquire about what's happening in their world outside of work too — take an interest in the daughter who just graduated high school, or the progress they're making on their home remodeling project, or their pride and joy over a new grandbaby.

When trying out the VIP method, remember that visibility, interac- tion, and meaningful probing conversations exist on a two-way street. If you want your people to open up to you, you'll have to open up to them. Daily "face time" with your team members is critical to gauging their pressure and stress. Most team members appreciate and admire leaders who are visible and interact with them on a personal level. Take the time daily to probe and find out what's going well and what's going wrong. Ask them if they have any concerns or are confused about anything. Again, ask how you can help.

Remember that visibility, interaction, and meaningful probing conversations exist on a two-way street. If you want your people to open up to you, you'll have to open up to them.

Reflection Question for Lesson 2: How would you define your relationship with your team members?

_____

_____

_____

_____

_____

_____

 Time for a break! When you're ready, move ahead to another chapter/lesson and then come back to the following START Activity and Passport exercise during your second read-through of the book.

START Activity

Try out the VIP method and make it your own.

1. Work with your leadership mentor to complete Part B of the Leadership Education & Application Passport.

2. Your Target Outcome is to engage each direct report within your department each day of the next week by being visible, by interacting with them and by asking them probing questions to develop a deeper relationship. When I do this activity, I put one Jolly Rancher candy in my shirt pocket for each direct report. At the beginning of each engagement, I shake hands and give each person a piece of candy. The candy is a nice gesture and it's a fun way to keep track of your daily engagements. If you have candy left over at the end of the day, you have to try harder the next day. Think of a fun way to adapt such a practice for remote workers too; being physically in the same space isn't a requirement for meaningful connection.

3. After each engagement, make a note of any significant comments made by the team member, like a child's birthday on Saturday. This will give you something specific to follow up on the *next* time you meet.

4. At the end of the week, follow up with your own leadership mentor to complete Part B of the Leadership Education & Application Passport, which follows.

Leadership Education & Application Passport

Part A – *Work with your leadership mentor to complete the Target Outcome and Actions sections below.*

Skill: Building Remarkable Team-Member Relationships

Target Outcome: With whom will you be applying this skill and what are you hoping to accomplish by using this skill?

_____

_____

_____

Actions: What actions need to be taken before and during the application of this skill?

- _____

- _____

- _____

- _____

- _____

Part B – *Take time with your leadership mentor to review the results of your actions and what you took away from this experience. Look for ways to improve your next experience using this skill.*

Results:

- _____

- _____

- _____

- _____

- _____

Takeaways:

- _____

- _____

- _____

- _____

- _____

Once you have completed Parts A and B above, have your leadership mentor initial and date the stamp for this Lesson.

Congratulations! You are one step closer to being the leader you've always dreamed of being.

LEADERSHIP EDUCATION & APPLICATION PASSPORT

Initials: _____
Date: _____

★ CONTINUE 2 IMPROVE ★

"He who does not trust enough will not be trusted."

— *Lao Tzu*

Let Go of the Leash

Developing Trust in Your Team

Giving people more responsibility for making decisions in their jobs generates greater productivity, morale, and commitment. So why are leaders reluctant to let go of the leash?

Giving people more responsibility for making decisions in their jobs generates greater productivity, morale and commitment. So why are leaders reluctant to let go of the leash?

It's my experience that their reticence comes from one (or more) of just three common conditions:

- They think no one can do the work as well as they can.

- They feel they may no longer be needed if their team members excel at responsibilities the leader used to hoard just for himself or herself.

- They haven't developed enough trust in their team members.

The first two concerns are self-esteem issues, and the third is all about trust. We often hear that leaders need to earn the trust of their team members and very little about how leaders can learn to trust their team members. In this chapter, you will discover how to let go of the leash and trust your team.

We often hear that leaders need to earn the trust of their team members and very little about how leaders can learn to trust their team members.

In my 20s and 30s, I was actively involved in protection dog training, and even some 20 years later, I still catch the occasional dog. I love playing the role of the suspect, because I get to catch the dog. Imagine the adrenaline rush as a 60-pound mouth full of large white teeth comes barreling down on you at 30 miles an hour.

That was the rush I was anticipating again when, years after my formal volunteer work in dog training, I pestered a police officer into letting me catch his dog at the Fourth of July festival in my wife's hometown. Imagine my disappointment when I saw the officer was pulling on the leash with two hands while leaning backward instead of letting go of the leash. It wasn't until the dog was a couple feet from me that the officer allowed any slack in the leash. That poor dog was so tethered that he couldn't truly do his job.

The Trust Trap — No Shared Definition

What exactly does "catch" mean? This particular police officer and I had different definitions. I thought it meant the dog chasing me at full speed, teeth gnashing, ready to take me down. But the K-9 handler thought it meant "approach slowly and let the dog grab the arm wrap."

Those two definitions are incompatible. And they are both true. Now imagine my dog-catching experience as a metaphor for workplace interactions and trust from leaders regarding their people. Without a clear expectation from the leader, the team member stands a good chance of being disappointed, just as I was. Not letting your employees enjoy full experiences, risks, achievements, and visibility for the work they do is going to leave them feeling disenchanted — unmotivated and untrusted. This, in turn, will reduce morale, productivity, and commitment. Even worse, as long as the leader and team member have two different definitions of the work and their roles, they can never learn to trust each other.

Trust is faith that someone will not take advantage of you, especially when the other person hasn't demonstrated reliability or trustworthiness. When team members don't feel trusted, workplace productivity and engagement often suffer. It's up to leaders to signal trust in their team members in consistent and considerate ways.

When team members don't feel trusted, workplace productivity and engagement often suffer. It's up to leaders to signal trust in their team members in consistent and considerate ways.

Team members who feel trusted are higher performers, going above and beyond their roles and responsibilities. When they feel their leaders trust them to get the job done, they have greater confidence in the organization as a whole.

Trust is a two-way street. Just as the leader must earn the trust of his or her team members, team members must earn the trust of their leaders. Leaders fall into one of three levels of trust when it comes to handing over projects to their team members.

1. There are those who always hold the leash tight while pulling back.

2. There are those who hold a loose leash.

3. And there are those who let go of the leash.

The first level — those who hold tight and frequently pull back on the leash — are (more often than not) insecure. These are leaders who don't think anyone can do the task or job as well as they can. They may also worry that if they let go, they will no longer be needed.

Trust levels 2 and 3 are given by confident leaders based on the leader's perception of each team member's skills and abilities when it comes to a particular task. A leader exhibiting level 2 trust provides the team member with specific goals and objectives. Once the objective is clear, the leader defines the level of freedom he or she is prepared to give the team member when it comes to making decisions or spending organizational budget. Anything outside of those boundaries requires the team member to check in with the leader.

When a team member has earned level 3 trust, it's usually because the leader feels the team member has the skills, abilities, and confidence to handle the project with little to no oversight. Typically, the team member is given a goal and left on their own to accomplish the task. Their only responsibility is to achieve the goal and communicate the project status at regular intervals.

Leaders must have what is known as cognitive trust in their team members before they can extend level 2 or 3 trust. Cognitive trust depends on the leader's appraisal of the team member's competence, reliability, and confidence. Leaders adjust their level of trust based on the team member's track record. They look at a team member's commitment to the organizational goals and objectives.

So, let's revisit the story about the community festival and the K-9 I was prepared to tangle with. As it turned out, the K-9 (the proverbial job or task if we follow the workplace metaphor to a fault) wasn't the problem; it was the officer who wouldn't cooperate. What did his actions say about his perception of my skills and abilities? His actions told me he did not trust that I could take a full-throttle hit from his dog, aptly named Chase. An even better question is, what could the officer have done to create a better and more rewarding experience for me?

Remember that if the leader's expectations of responsibility are less than that of the team member themselves, the team member will walk away feeling disappointed and cheated — just as I did at the Fourth of July festival. Of course, community police officers have a responsibility not to hurt random citizens at holiday festivals, so I understand why he was overly cautious. But in the workplace, the relationships should be strong enough that leaders can loosen the leash. When leaders assign projects, they must ensure the team member is clear about their level of responsibility. And once they're sure, they need to let go ... and trust.

There is a saying that goes a little something like this: "If you break someone's trust, it is like crumpling up a perfect piece of paper. You can smooth it with your hand — you can even iron it — but it's never going to be the same again." I certainly agree that there are certain trusts that, once broken, can never be restored to perfection. One of your responsibilities as a leader is to avoid crumpling the paper.

What Leaders Can Do to Build Trust

When making assignments, it's crucial that leaders provide clear expectations. Setting clear expectations up front — including shared clarity about roles and responsibilities — ensures that there are no surprises. This takes the stress out of the daily routine. Don't assume that others know what you expect of them and don't assume that you're clear about their expectations of you.

Treat your team's mistakes and failures as opportunities to facilitate learning. If you've read Lesson 1 already, you know that I'm a strong proponent of leaders redefining what the word "failure" means. I teach all my clients that FAILURE is an acronym that stands for: **F**inding **A**nswers **i**n **L**ife **U**sing **R**eflective **E**valuation. You see, when we mess up or miss our target, we have an opportunity to reflect upon what happened, evaluate what went wrong and why, and walk away with answers that will serve us in many powerful ways in our careers and lives. Don't be afraid of failure — your own failures or those of your team members. Failure is human and it's full of opportunity to learn.

Don't be afraid of failure — your own failures or those of your team members. Failure is human and it's full of opportunity to learn.

Another surefire way to create and maintain trust is to communicate all the time. Lack of information creates assumptions (as well as fears and even paranoias) and undermines your team member's motivation and productivity. Always err on the side of overcommunicating.

Ultimately, trust leads to loyalty. And loyalty leads to people doing their best to deliver your expectations. To earn trust and respect, you have to give trust and respect — as well as look out for your team members. And if you do, there will be no limit to what your team can achieve.

Remember that, as a leader, your ultimate goal is to let go of the leash.

Reflection Question for Lesson 3: Where could you have let go and trusted more today, yesterday, or recently?

_____

_____

_____

_____

_____

_____

Time for a break! When you're ready, move ahead to another chapter/lesson and then come back to the following START Activity and Passport exercise during your second read-through of the book.

START Activity

Let go and trust.

1. Identify a project you can assign to a team member or group of team members.

2. Ask yourself: "What is the worst that can happen?"

3. Meet with the team member and take time to understand the team member's (or team members') expectations related to the task.

4. Explain your vision for the task and why that is your vision.

5. Create a plan that accomplishes the vision while allowing the team member(s) to meet their expectations over time.

6. After speaking with your team member(s), complete Part B of the following Leadership Education & Application Passport.

Leadership Education & Application Passport

Part A – *Work with your leadership mentor to complete the Target Outcome and Actions sections below.*

Skill: Developing Trust in Your Team

Target Outcome: What are you hoping to accomplish by practicing the skill of trusting your people, in general and as it relates to the specific situation you have identified?

_____

_____

_____

Actions: What actions need to be taken before and during the application of this skill to ensure a successful outcome?

- _____

- _____

- _____

- _____

- _____

Part B – *With your leadership mentor, review the results of your practice run at letting go of the leash. Examine what you took away from this experience and look for ways to improve your next experience when exercising trust with your team members.*

Results:

- _____
- _____
- _____
- _____
- _____

Takeaways:

- _____
- _____
- _____
- _____
- _____

Once you have completed Parts A and B above, have your leadership mentor initial and date the stamp for this Lesson.

Congratulations! You are one step closer to being the leader you've always dreamed of being.

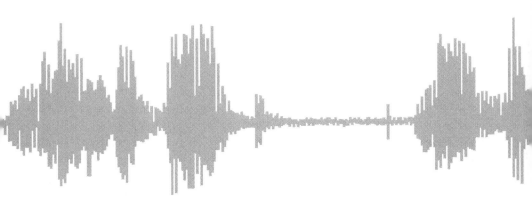

"When you show deep empathy toward others, their defensive energy goes down, and positive energy replaces it. That's when you can get more creative in solving problems."

— *Stephen Covey*

LESSON 4

SWITCH Gears

Avoiding Blame and Defensiveness

Have you ever been in a coaching conversation — where you were trying to provide feedback or a safe place for a team member to talk about their work — and felt like you were chasing your tail because the person you were attempting to coach couldn't focus on your concerns or dig deeply into the topic at hand? Maybe they were deflecting blame onto others or making excuses for work that wasn't completed fully, well, or on time. Or maybe they were preoccupied with something else. Either way, you might be able to relate to the frustrations of trying to coach someone in a moment they aren't able to receive the coaching. When the person you're coaching is just not able to stay focused on your issue, it's incredibly difficult to reach a resolution. So, what can you do?

Let me share a story about the frustrations of working in my current office, where this distracted "coachee" situation happened to me just the other day. I was in my office, trying to shoot a brief video when my next-door neighbor, Felix, started making lots of noise. When it became apparent that he wasn't going to stop anytime soon, I went outside to see if I could get him to be quiet. I implored him, using all my charms.

I didn't have any luck, at first. Felix is a good neighbor, but he's not human. He's a cute little brown Pitbull mix. I don't know if you've ever tried to have a coaching conversation with a dog; if you have, you know it isn't easy. Every time I said "quiet," he'd stop barking, look at me, and start barking again. After a few attempts, I noticed he kept looking over my shoulder. When I turned to see what was distracting him, I saw a gray plastic Lowes bag in the street, dancing in the wind. As soon as I dealt with the bag, I was able to get Felix to quiet down so I could shoot my video. Problem solved! Felix wasn't a bad boy; we just needed to deal with the distraction.

Unlike my situation with Felix, most of us (thankfully) speak the same language as our team members. However, that doesn't guarantee your coaching conversations will be successful. So, that begs the question, "What can we do to increase the chances of win-win outcomes while avoiding blame and defensiveness during our coaching conversations?"

It literally may require you to SWITCH gears. We've all been there before and you're guilty too. Someone is talking to us but our eyes are glazed over and we're thinking about something else. "Earth to Daniel!" In those situations, no matter how receptive we are to feedback, it can be impossible to hear what the other person is saying to us.

What can we do to increase the chances of win-win outcomes while avoiding blame and defensiveness during our coaching conversations? It literally may require you to SWITCH gears.

When you notice this distraction or disconnection among your people as a leader, you need to have the presence of mind to stop talking and focus on the other person's needs. SWITCH is a six-step process (State, Watch, Investigate, Treat, Change, Handle) for win-win coaching conversations. (I know you're loving all the acronyms, right? So am I! They help us remember important tools as we become stronger leaders.)

SWITCH – State | Watch | Investigate | Treat | Change | Handle

The first step in focusing on the other person's needs is called **"State."** State the situation using a "3-Part Factual Statement." Begin by clearly identifying the issue or point of failure. This is the tricky part because you want to focus on the problem not the person. The second element involves describing your emotional reaction to the person's failure. The last element requires sharing the source behind your emotional reaction.

Focus on the problem not the person.

3-Part Factual Statement Formula:

1. The ISSUE you observed

2. Your emotional REACTION to the issue

3. The SOURCE behind the emotion.

Here's an example of the 3-Part Factual Statement in action:

> "Bobby, I noticed the payroll wasn't entered by 11:00 a.m. on Monday *[ISSUE]*, and I get antsy *[REACTION]* because it doesn't give me much time to run all of the payroll reports before the noon transmittal deadline. *[SOURCE]*"

In this example, it is clear my focus was on the issue (i.e., the late payroll and the mad dash to finish the reports) and not on the person (Bobby). It also makes my emotional reaction clear to the team member and helps them understand the source of that emotion for me. Once you state the issue, stop talking and listen.

The next step in the SWITCH formula is **"Watch."** Watch for clues and cues that the team member is distracted by some other issue or concern. These clues and cues can be verbal, visual, or both. It's your job as a leader to notice when the team member is out of sorts.

During the coaching conversation, a team member might say something like, "Yeah, I'll add that to the list." If you take that statement literally, you'd have no reason to think it would not be accomplished. However, if the tone of voice and body language are not compatible with that statement (i.e., if the person seems to be conveying sarcasm or frustration), you could be disappointed in the outcome. Taking the time to notice these subtleties will make it possible for you to get to the desired outcome faster.

We've all heard the phrase, "Leave work at work and home at home." Sounds good but it's impossible unless you were born with a switch you can toggle back and forth labeled "work" and "home." During the coaching conversation, it's important for you to accept the fact that we all have personal baggage that makes its way into our workplace. We don't and can't ask employees to check their humanity at the door. Ultimately, that's a good thing.

The next step in the SWITCH formula then is **"Investigate."** Investigate the worker's issues or concerns with REAL listening. (Yep! Another awesome acronym!)

- *Reflect* on the possible hidden meaning behind their words or actions.

- *Engage* the team member with questions to get clarification.

- *Analyze* the reason behind the team member's distraction or concerns.

- *Linger* long enough to think about their answers before speaking again.

Taking the time to watch and investigate is what distinguishes a person with the title "leader" and a "true leader." True leaders care about the team members they lead and know the importance of building remarkable working relationships.

True leaders care about the team members they lead and know the importance of building remarkable working relationships.

Next up in the SWITCH formula is **"Treat."** Treat the worker's issue or concern. I'm not saying it's your responsibility as a leader to solve your team member's personal problems. I'm saying you need to be able to recognize when a team member's personal problems are affecting the workplace. Your responsibility as a leader in these situations is to guide the team member to the resources that can help them solve their own personal problems. And if the issue is not personal, but is procedural or related to people problems in the organization, it's your job as a leader to clear away those obstacles by fixing processes and procedures or getting others aligned and on board so your team member can resolve their issue. If the problem at hand is something the team member needs to address on their own, be sure to get their commitment to take action on their personal problem before moving on to the next step in the SWITCH process. And if the problem needs your attention, *you* should commit to jumping in to help right away.

The next step in the SWITCH formula is **"Change."** Change the course of the conversation. Now that you've helped the team member with their issue or concern, it's time for you to refocus their attention on your original concern regarding their performance. Restate the issue in a non-judgmental, blameless, and factual manner. Refer back to the "State" process for help in doing this.

Finally, the SWITCH formula is completed with a step called **"Handle."** Handle your original performance issue by defining and getting agreement on the necessary actions. Always ask the team member for their thoughts on how they can meet your performance expectations. It's important to note that not all their ideas will be good ideas. That topic is covered in Lesson 21: "Responding to Bad Ideas." But often, your team members will have brilliant solutions to their own problems. Let them lead the charge where they can.

Using the SWITCH Formula — Here, There, and Everywhere

Keep in mind that this process is not limited to just your coaching conversations with your team members. You can also use this with your children, significant other, or a friend. This process can also work if you are talking to your boss. Let's say your boss is distracted by another issue and can't focus on what you have to say. If you apply the SWITCH process, not only will you be able to convey your message, you just might be able to help your boss with an issue. Indeed, SWITCH is a formula that helps you coach up, down, and across organizations, families, and communities.

In the end, we're all a little bit like Felix, the dog. We all have baggage that affects how we perform at work, and we're all prone to distractions even on our best days. Coaching conversations are a critical part of leadership. The ability to effortlessly SWITCH gears back and forth between your concerns and the concerns of your team members will greatly increase your win-win ratio.

Reflection Question for Lesson 4: When something didn't go as planned, did you focus on the issue or the person?

_____

_____

_____

_____

_____

_____

Time for a break! When you're ready, move ahead to another chapter/lesson and then come back to the following START Activity and Passport exercise during your second read-through of the book.

START Activity

Apply the SWITCH process when delivering performance coaching.

Here are your action steps for this chapter:

1. Identify a performance issue being faced by a team member.

2. Work with your leadership mentor to structure a non-blameful 3-Part Factual Statement before the coaching session and complete Part A of the Leadership Education & Application Passport.

3. Apply the SWITCH process when delivering performance coaching.

4. After the coaching session, complete Part B of the Leadership Education & Application Passport on the following pages.

Leadership Education & Application Passport

Part A – *Work with your leadership mentor to complete the Target Outcome and Actions sections below.*

Skill: Avoiding Blame and Defensiveness

Target Outcome: Say a few words about the person with whom you will be applying the SWITCH skill and what you are hoping to accomplish by using this skill.

_____

_____

_____

_____

Actions: What actions need to be taken before and during the application of this skill?

- _____
- _____
- _____
- _____
- _____

Part B – *With your leadership mentor, review the results of your initial test of the SWITCH formula (and/or REAL listening). Examine what you took away from this experience and look for ways to improve your next experience when avoiding blame and defensiveness with your team members.*

Results:

- _____
- _____
- _____
- _____

Takeaways:

- _____
- _____
- _____
- _____

Once you have completed Parts A and B above, have your leadership mentor initial and date the stamp for this Lesson.

Congratulations! You are one step closer to being the leader you've always dreamed of being.

"When you explain to people what you're trying to do, as opposed to just making demands or delegating tasks, you can build instant trust."

— *Simon Sinek*

It's Not Just About Your Kite

Making Productive Requests

When I was seven years old, I learned two very important leadership lessons that would come to serve me well many years later. Let me take you back ... It was a very windy summer afternoon — a "let's go fly a kite" kind of day. I was flying my kite, a black and yellow bat kite with its big bloodshot eyes looking down on me. Out of nowhere, a strong gust of wind hit the kite and broke the string. I watched as my big black and yellow bat, untethered from my control, fell to the ground a block away from where I stood. I went running to retrieve it and when I rounded the corner, there were three other boys standing around my kite. When I told them it was mine, they said, "Not anymore" — and the fight was on. I didn't win but I held my own. When I got home, kiteless, and told my step-dad what had happened, he said, "I'm proud of you for standing up for yourself and what was yours. I'll buy you a new kite on my way home from work tomorrow."

The next day, I ran to the door and almost pulled the door out of my step-dad's hand and said, all in one breath, "Where is my kite? Is it in the car? Can I go get it?" He said, "No, you may not. Not until you can learn to ask for it the right way." I knew not to push my luck and I retreated for the night.

When my step-dad pulled into the driveway the *next* day, I was waiting for him when he walked in the door. I said, "Sir, may I go get my kite out of the car?" He said, "No, not until you can be more considerate. You didn't even ask me how I was. You only cared about the kite."

I was listening and I was learning. Attempt number three took place the next day. This time, I waited on the couch until my step-dad had a chance to put his things away and grab a beer. I tried not to look too eager or be too pushy. I said, "How was your day?" He said, "It was fine; thank you for asking. Would you like to get your kite out of the car and fly it?"

A ha! I had finally figured out how to get what I wanted while being respectful of the person I was asking. Words matter! Impactful and meaningful word choice, paired with consideration for the other person's feelings, are key factors for making effective requests that get results.

Words matter! Impactful and meaningful word choice, paired with consideration for the other person's feelings, are key factors for making effective requests that get results.

Here are six tips to help you make more effective requests. A good way to remember them after you've learned them is to think of them as the "Six C's."

1. **Be Considerate**

When I was growing up, I was taught to always say *yes ma'am, no ma'am* and *yes sir, no sir* as well as *please* and *thank you*. I still say those words today because I firmly believe that having good manners and being polite means going out of your way to make other people feel at ease and respected. It may sound simple, but a well-placed "please" or "thank you" goes a long way to boosting your reputation as a leader.

Having good manners and being polite means going out of your way to make other people feel at ease and respected.

Another form of consideration is making sure you don't overwhelm your team members by placing too much on their plates. Sometimes you have to be willing to take something off their plates or postpone other deadlines until the more pressing matter is complete. By respecting other people's time, you show that you value them. And an added bonus to exercise such consideration and respect is that your colleagues may, as a result, feel more inclined to make an extra effort in the future.

2. **Clarify Your Request**

When making a request, it's important to first think through what you want to say so you don't leave out any critical information. If you provide your audience with incomplete information, they will begin to fill in the gaps with assumptions, which may be significantly different from your desired outcome or intent.

To ensure clarity before making a request, ask yourself the following questions:

- What is the reason I'm making this request?
- What is the specific outcome I am trying to achieve?

- When does this request need to be completed?
- How much money is budgeted for this request?
- How frequently do I want to be updated and what should be included in the updates?

3. **Communicate Your Request**

   It's always important to have your audience's full attention before making your request. Start by putting the other person (or people) at ease and remove distractions. This may require moving to another area or meeting room to limit noise and potential interruptions. The tone of your voice matters, especially when you are asking someone to do something they may not enjoy doing.

   Don't make sloppy requests. You've probably had someone say something like, "I need someone to make handouts for the presentation later today." (Do you hear how vague that is, and how many other questions will be required for follow-up? I can picture it now, all the hands going up or the mumbling in confusion.) Don't put the responsibility for clarifying who, when, and where on those people in the room. Hinting or being vague is inconsiderate and not very "leader like." If you want Jacob to print and staple 35 sets of handouts and put them on the conference room chairs before 2:00 p.m., then say so explicitly.

4. **Check Understanding**

   One of the most common mistakes made when making a request is assuming your audience understands what you want. The other person's ability to clearly see your desired outcome is the most important factor in determining success or failure.

   There are three things you should do to ensure understanding. First, ask the other person to share their understanding of your request using their own words. Try saying something like, "Okay, let's recap. Walk me through what you're going to do." (Perhaps even gesturing to the notebook where they've been taking notes as a cue for them to articulate what they wrote down during the conversation.) Second, ask specific questions to ensure they understand all aspects of the request. And third, ask them if they have any additional questions or concerns.

One of the most common mistakes made when making a request is assuming your audience understands what you want. The other person's ability to clearly see your desired outcome is the most important factor in determining success or failure.

---

5. **Confirm Commitment**

No matter how well the other person understands your request, there is no guarantee they will follow through on the request — fully, on time, with quality work, or at all. Many leaders have assumed that the other person has accepted the task only to find the deadline has come and gone and no action has been taken. The easiest way to get a commitment is to simply ask the other person if they will commit to taking on the task and completing it on time. When most people give their word, they feel compelled to follow through.

You are obviously looking for that person to give a solid *yes* but that doesn't always happen. If you get any other answer, don't be thrown; put on your listening hat. Go back to the first "C" — consideration. It's not just about you; find out what their concerns are and work to overcome them.

6. **Create Accountability**

As I said earlier, most people will follow through once they've given their word. That doesn't mean other things won't get in the way of that commitment. For that reason, you must have an accountability plan in place to ensure the task is moving ahead as planned. Check in regularly on long-term projects, and hold your people accountable for the commitments they have made.

At work (and in life), our experiences, our measurable results, and our overall satisfaction often stem from projects and interactions that started with an "ask" — an assignment, a request, a favor, a need. As such, mastering the art of making requests is a workplace and leadership superpower. If you want to make strong requests that get you the results you desire, try following the 6 C's formula for making productive requests.

Reflection Question for Lesson 5: What are some examples of how you showed consideration for your team members today?

_____

_____

_____

_____

_____

Time for a break! When you're ready, move ahead to another chapter/lesson and then come back to the following START Activity and Passport exercise during your second read-through of the book.

START Activity

Ask a team member to perform a task they don't normally do.

- Be Considerate – Find out what their current obligations are and the urgency of each.

- Clarify the Request (by answering the following questions):

    - What is the reason I'm making this request?

    - What is the specific outcome I'm trying to achieve?

    - When does this request need to be completed?

    - How much money is budgeted for this request?

    - How frequently do I want to be updated and what should be included in the updates?

- Communicate Request

- Check Understanding

- Confirm Commitment

- Create Accountability.

Leadership Education & Application Passport

Part A – *Work with your leadership mentor to complete the Target Outcome and Actions sections below.*

Skill: Making Productive Requests

Target Outcome: With whom will you be applying this skill and what are you hoping to accomplish by using this skill?

_____

_____

_____

_____

Actions: What actions need to be taken before and during the application of this skill?

- _____

- _____

- _____

- _____

- _____

Part B – *With your leadership mentor, review the results of your initial test of the 6 C's formula for making requests. Examine what you took away from this experience and look for ways to improve your next experience when making requests of your team members.*

Results:

- _____
- _____
- _____
- _____
- _____

Takeaways:

- _____
- _____
- _____
- _____
- _____

Once you have completed Parts A and B above, have your leadership mentor initial and date the stamp for this Lesson.

Congratulations! You are one step closer to being the leader you've always dreamed of being.

"If the worker hasn't learned, the instructor hasn't taught."

— *TWI Job Instruction Motto*

Avoiding the Garland Effect

Providing Training That Develops Confidence and Competence

Do you know where you were on October 5, 1982, at 0200 hours? I know some of you weren't even born yet, but I was standing in the turret of an armored vehicle in my Air Force fatigues with an M-60 ammo belt wrapped around me like Christmas tree garland. To understand what I'm talking about, we need to go back in time 30 minutes to 0130 hours on October 5, 1982. I was part of a four-man Fireteam assigned to the bomber alert area at Minot Air Force Base in North Dakota. We had just returned from a terrorist threat exercise initiated by a base-wide Operational Readiness Inspection (ORI).

The inspectors were waiting for us in our secure facility to assess our knowledge and readiness. We were knocking it out of the park, question after question, when one inspector asked, "Who is responsible for the M-60?" I said, "I am, Sir." He shot a few questions my way that I easily answered. Then he said, "Let's go in the garage and have you man the M-60 mounted to the turret." Once I was in position, he said, "Airman Matthews, half-load the M-60." So, I opened a can of ammo, set it on the roof of the armored vehicle, and inserted the ammo belt. Then he said, "I need you to do one more thing. Turn the turret clockwise 360 degrees." As soon as he said those words, I knew I was screwed. You see, I'd never been trained how to fire an M-60 from the turret of an armored vehicle, which means I'd never learned how to mount the ammo can on the turret.

Now picture this. The ammo can is on the roof below me (a flat, stationary surface) and I'm in a turret that rotates. As I turn (and the ammo can doesn't), the ammo belt wraps around me like Christmas tree garland. Not only did I feel stupid and embarrassed, I single-handedly wiped out all the high marks we'd received up to that point. We were all relieved of our Fireteam responsibilities and sent to other posts, where we would have to work another 12 hours without sleep.

The leadership lesson here comes when we ask the question: How could my failure have been avoided? I'd been trained in deployment tactics and how to fire the M-60 machine gun, but I'd never been trained on the simple, yet critical, task of mounting the ammo can on the turret. Whether you lead in the military or in a Fortune 500 company, your training program will vary depending on the exact type of work your team members perform.

There is a difference between the work performed by someone on the manufacturing floor and someone in the office sitting at a desk working on a computer. However, there are best practices that will apply regardless of the job, environment, or tools used to perform the job. The three most important things to keep in mind when seeking to provide training that develops confidence and competence are:

- Knowledge Types

- Teaching Method

- Long Jobs

Let me break it down for you.

Knowledge Types

Knowledge on the job falls roughly into three categories:

- *Core tasks* are the main duties and responsibilities your team members perform on a daily basis.

- *Procedural knowledge* includes standard operating procedures (SOPs), policies, company values, vision, and mission statements. Introducing these early in the onboarding process helps to establish your company culture and the attitude of your new hires.

- *Peripheral tasks* are minor or rarely performed tasks that, while often overlooked in training, can result in failure if not performed when needed (like how to mount an M-60 ammo can on a turret!).

Teaching Method

A program created in the 1940s to help American manufacturers meet the needs of the war effort provides a perfect outline for delivering training safely, correctly, and consistently. The program was called TWI Job Instruction and consisted of four phases: prepare worker, present operation, try out performance, and follow up.

Prepare Worker

Learning a new job — whether you are a new hire or a seasoned employee — can be a stressful time. To make the learning process easier, it is important that you take some time to prepare the worker to learn. This means putting them at ease before jumping into the training.

Once the worker is at ease, you need to let the worker/learner know what you will be teaching and find out what the worker may already know about the task or topic at hand, so you don't waste time covering information they're already familiar with. The last step you need to take to prepare the worker to learn is get them interested in the job by letting them know the importance of the job.

Present Operation

In the second phase of teaching, you are showing the worker how to do the job over several repetitions while progressively providing three types of information:

- Major Steps – Value-added logical segments that advance the job.

- Key Points – Information that explains how to do a job.

- Reasons – An explanation of why the worker needs to do each key point.

Try Out Performance

In this phase of the training process, the worker performs the job while you provide coaching and correct any errors. Just as you did in the previous phase, the worker will perform the task multiple times while progressively proving the three types of information.

Follow Up

Once the learner has demonstrated a basic level of competence, you can step back from supervising the worker. Let them know they will not be on their own, though, by designating someone other than yourself to whom they can go for help. Encourage them to ask questions. Let them know you will check on them frequently and the frequency of checking will taper off as their competence increases.

Long Jobs

Aside from knowledge types and teaching method, the third thing to keep in mind when developing strong training programs is the reality of what I call "long jobs." Some jobs consist of several tasks and cannot be taught all at once. Teaching lengthy multi-layered jobs can become confusing to the learner, so the best approach in these situations is to break down the job into manageable chunks.

Once you've divided the job into chunks, you need to classify each chunk based on its level of complexity using simple, moderate, and complex categories. When teaching these chunks, you will follow the "simple to complex" method. This means the job may not be taught in a linear fashion and that the training exercise might require that the learner focus only on the simple tasks (or chunks) first, while an experienced worker performs the more complex portions of the job not being taught just yet. These bite-sized chunks are taught using the same four-phase teaching method explained earlier (i.e., prepare worker, present operation, try out performance, and follow up). It's how the teaching method is applied that is different. In the diagram here, you will see how the process and the chunks are combined to train the person safely, correctly, and consistently.

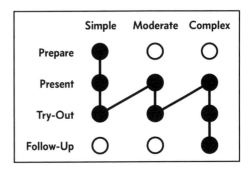

Well-rounded leaders are also good trainers. Your job as a leader is to make your team members successful. To do that, you need to ensure they have all the information necessary to perform their jobs success-fully. Don't let your team members feel like a Christmas tree wrapped in garland — that was enough embarrassment for all of us!

Well-rounded leaders are also good trainers.

Reflection Question for Lesson 6: Which jobs or tasks in your department(s) are the most difficult to master and how many of your team members can perform those tasks expertly?

Time for a break! When you're ready, move ahead to another chapter/lesson and then come back to the following START Activity and Passport exercise during your second read-through of the book.

START Activity

Identify the three types of knowledge (core, procedural, and peripheral).

1. Identify a simple task that one of your team members performs.

2. Locate the SOPs or other documents used to train team members on the task.

3. Review those documents and see if you can identify the three types of knowledge.

4. Work with the team member responsible for the task to update any missing information from their previous training.

5. Train the rest of your team on the three types of knowledge and have them update task documents to include any missing information.

Leadership Education & Application Passport

Part A – *Work with your leadership mentor to complete the Target Outcome and Actions sections below.*

Skill: Providing Training That Develops Confidence and Competence

Target Outcome: With whom will you be applying your new training skills and what are you hoping to accomplish?

Actions: What actions need to be taken before and during the application of this skill?

-
-
-
-
-

Part B – *With your leadership mentor, review the results of your experiments in providing better training. Examine what you took away from this experience and look for ways to improve your next experience when attempting to develop confidence and competence in your workers.*

Results:

- _____

- _____

- _____

- _____

- _____

Takeaways:

- _____

- _____

- _____

- _____

- _____

Once you have completed Parts A and B above, have your leadership mentor initial and date the stamp for this Lesson.

Congratulations! You are one step closer to being the leader you've always dreamed of being.

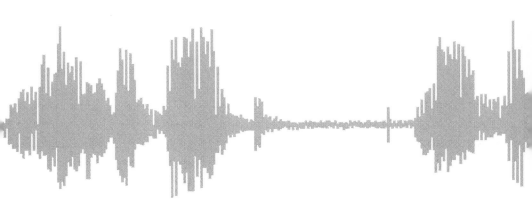

"Having no problems is the biggest problem of all."

— *Taiichi Ohno*

Seeing with Four Sights, Not Four Eyes

Embracing Four Problem-Solving Types

Did you get chased around the school yard while being called "four eyes" because you wore glasses? If you did, we have something in common. But as leaders, we all need to have something else in common and that is the Problem-Solving Four Sights. Without the four sights of effective problem-solving, you can be blindsided by customer complaints, inefficiencies, repeat problems, and competitors who pass you by like you're standing still. Your ability to solve a wide variety of problems depends on visual acuity and your field of view.

Without the four sights of effective problem-solving, you can be blindsided by customer complaints, inefficiencies, repeat problems and competitors who pass you by like you're standing still.

Visual acuity refers to clarity of vision. Leaders need to understand their organization's goals and objectives in order to contribute to the success of the organization. Field of view is similar to your peripheral vision: it's everything outside of your central vision. The acuity of your peripheral vision gets substantially worse as you get farther from the central vision. As a leader, your foundation for problem-solving, continuous improvement, and innovation is directly linked to knowing when and how to look directly in front of you, into the future, or beyond whatever you thought was possible. There's a reason why we use the figurative term "vision" when referring to a leader's plans and ambitions for his or her organization. Articulating, honing, and caring for that vision requires an understanding of the "problem-solving four sights" — a method for seeing what's really happening so you can perform at your best.

Problem-Solving Four Sights

- Clear Sight

- Fore Sight

- HIND Sight

- X-ray Sight

The first level of problem solving — **Clear Sight** — is about having a measurable, shared standard. It requires high visual acuity with a narrow field of view. This is the ability to look at what is directly in front of you today and compare it to a standard to determine if an abnormal suboptimal condition exists. Ideally, Clear Sight requires clearly defined standards that have been shared and agreed to by the entire organization, otherwise known as key performance indicators (KPIs). If your company does not have KPIs, you can still apply Clear Sight within your department.

Start by establishing clear standards for the quality of the products or services your department is responsible for. Also set standards for safety, productivity, and cost savings. This will allow you to look at a given situation and know if a problem exists. If you are in human resources, for example, a KPI could be the employee turnover rate. The purchasing department, on the other hand, might measure purchase-order cycle times, and operations/manufacturing could track on-time shipping of customer orders.

A problem is defined as the difference or gap between the standard and the current situation. In regard to Clear Sight, something has happened to cause the problem and a formal problem-solving process (like the one described in my book *The A3 Workbook: Unlock Your Problem-Solving Mind*) is required in order to find and eliminate the root cause of the problem.

The second level of problem-solving — **Fore Sight** — entails having moderate visual acuity and a moderate field of view. This is about the ability to look at what is directly in front of you and, instead of looking back at

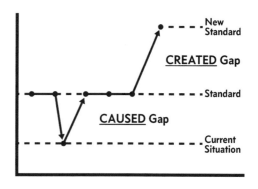

a standard (as you did with Clear Sight), being able to see the opportunity to take the work to a higher level in the near future (otherwise known as "continuous improvement"). Once a KPI has been stable for a significant period, it might be time to raise the bar by creating a new, higher standard. In Fore Sight, instead of looking for the root cause, you are identifying and eliminating the barriers and obstacles that stand in your way of achieving the new standard.

The third level of problem-solving — **HIND Sight** — combines low visual acuity with a wide field of view while looking in the rearview mirror. What this means is that you take a wide view of the overall process to look at the positives and negatives at the end of the project and apply those learnings to future projects. In other words, HIND Sight is about seeing the past to avoid future problems. The acronym HIND stands for Hastening Input of Necessary Data. HIND involves sitting down with your team and stakeholders soon after the completion of a project to conduct reflective evaluation. The discussion should center around what went well, what could be repeated next time, what went wrong, and what to avoid during the next project.

The fourth level of problem-solving — **X-ray Sight** — is all about creativity. It begins with very low visual acuity and an extremely wide field of view. X-ray Sight is about having no idea of what is possible but being open to all possibilities. Mastering X-ray Sight involves the ability to create new, innovative, and creative ideas, processes, and products by asking "stupid" questions and having the courage to explore beyond your boundaries, barriers, and biases.

Our thoughts and perceptions about what is possible combine to form an impenetrable sphere around us. What most people don't know is that they have the ability for X-ray Sight or X-ray vision. Two great examples of organizations with X-ray Sight are Uber and Airbnb. Both companies not only asked the stupid question

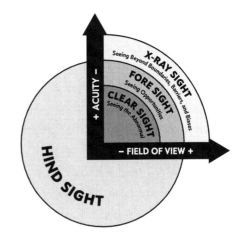

they had the courage to explore the possibility. In Uber's case, they asked, "How can we run a taxi service without having to purchase any taxis?" Airbnb did something equally game-changing when they asked, "How can we run hotels around the world without building a single hotel?"

Asking the stupid question is the easy part. It's having the courage to explore the stupid question and make it a reality that drives innovation. There is no better example than skydiver Luke Aikins. He jumped out of a plane from 25,000 feet without a parachute or wingsuit and lived to tell the story. He simply took a page from the trapeze artist handbook — he fell into a 100-foot-by-100-foot net suspended 200 feet above the ground.

There are people who will discourage you, tell you there is no way, and flat-out laugh at you. Just like fellow skydiver Michael Turoff did when he said it was a ridiculously dangerous stunt that could have easily resulted in Luke's death.

When you ask the stupid question, you need to make sure that your team has a clear understanding of what you are trying to accomplish. In his book, *Think Big, Act Bigger*, Jeffrey Hayzlett, former Eastman Kodak CMO and the host of C-Suite with Jeffrey Hayzlett, tells a story about asking his team to boost his Facebook and Twitter fans by 25,000. They came back with a plan that would fall 10,000 fans short of his goal. When he asked why the plan was only for 15,000 fans, they replied, "the budget." Most people would have been satisfied with that answer but not Jeffrey. Instead, he said, "I never gave you a budget. I asked what it would take."

If you want to excel in leadership, you must be able to do more than just remedy customer complaints — you must prevent them. Every day at work, you should be looking to reduce process inefficiencies, prevent repeat problems, and find ways to outpace your competitors. Understanding and applying the Four Sights will take you a long way toward succeeding in all three areas.

Reflection Question for Lesson 7: What problems did you face today?

_____

_____

_____

_____

Time for a break! When you're ready, move ahead to another chapter/lesson and then come back to the following START Activity and Passport exercise during your second read-through of the book.

START Activity

Apply X-ray Sight to trigger innovation on your team.

1. Ask your team a stupid question or have them ask a stupid question about one of your processes.

2. Have the courage to give your team the time to find a possible answer, even if it is only 10 minutes a day.

3. Regardless of the outcome, have them present their findings.

Leadership Education & Application Passport

Part A – *Work with your leadership mentor to complete the Target Outcome and Actions sections below.*

Skill: Embracing Four Problem-Solving Types

Target Outcome: With whom will you be applying this skill and what are you hoping to accomplish?

_____

_____

_____

_____

Actions: What actions need to be taken before and during the application of this skill?

- _____

- _____

- _____

- _____

- _____

Part B – *With your leadership mentor, review the results of your problem-solving efforts using one or more of the "Sights." Examine what you took away from this experience and look for ways to improve your next experience in problem-solving by looking at situations through a new lens.*

Results:

- _____
- _____
- _____
- _____
- _____

Takeaways:

- _____
- _____
- _____
- _____
- _____

Once you have completed Parts A and B above, have your leadership mentor initial and date the stamp for this Lesson.

Congratulations! You are one step closer to being the leader you've always dreamed of being.

LEADERSHIP EDUCATION & APPLICATION PASSPORT

Initials: _____
Date: _____

★ CONTINUE 2 IMPROVE ★

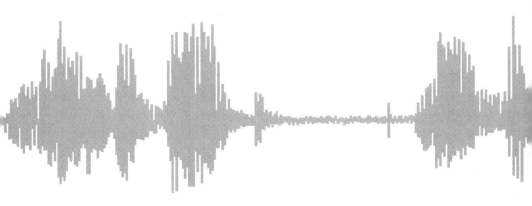

"Diversity and inclusion, which are the real grounds for creativity, must remain at the center of what we do."

— *Marco Bizzarri*

Performance Before Pedigree

Selecting the Right Players

When I was vacationing in Alaska, we visited an Iditarod dog sled training camp, where we got to get up close to the sled dogs. When the woman giving the presentation asked for questions, I said, "All of these dogs are different colors, sizes, hair coats, and breeds. They're obviously not huskies. What are they?"

I could tell by the look of disapproval on the presenter's face that I was about to be put in my place. She said, "The Alaskan husky is not considered a pure breed. You are thinking of the Siberian husky or the Alaskan malamute. An Alaskan husky is bred for speed and endurance whereas "Sibs," as we call them, are bred to conform to an American Kennel Club standard for appearance and must be able to prove their pedigree. Think of the difference between Alaskan huskies and Siberian huskies this way: one is selected based on its ability to perform, and the other is bred to look good on a couch. Alaskan huskies are not defined by a standard; they are defined by their *purpose* and *ability*. They must be able to quickly and efficiently pull a musher and 200-pound sled 938 miles through blizzards, whiteout conditions, gale-force winds, and sub-zero temperatures with wind chills reaching minus 100 degrees Fahrenheit."

Whoa. That's some dog!

I had just been schooled in "pedigree versus performance." And it was a lesson we can all apply at work, even if we don't train dogs for the Iditarod. Ask yourself, "How many times do we judge a person based on our implicit biases created by our own preference for a particular "pedigree" (of higher education, industry credentials, professional experience, etc.), instead of how well their skills and abilities meet our needs?" Our implicit bias can cause us to focus more on pedigree than performance. Our implicit bias influences how we make decisions, how we behave, and what we believe.

Implicit bias is universal. It's a biological function that helped early humans feel safe and it exists in all of us. So, the question is: How do we reduce the impacts of our implicit biases? The answer is simple: We need to wear Implicit Bias Blinders. Easily said, but the execution can be difficult.

By reading this book, you have already committed to doing the hard, thoughtful work of becoming a better leader. You're already in a good position to do the messy work of examining your implicit biases. And we're in it together. We all must challenge the assumptions behind our beliefs. We need to evaluate the criteria we use to select job candidates (or give high-visibility assignments) to ensure those we choose will contribute to our team's success. If we fail in this regard, we will only achieve mediocre results. We need to ask questions that help us determine what a candidate can add to our team's overall skill set. And we need to have humility through this process. Our implicit biases find their way into all aspects of leadership — including who we hire, how performance is evaluated, who we include on our project teams, how we dispense discipline, and who we promote.

Our implicit biases find their way into all aspects of leadership — including who we hire, how performance is evaluated, who we include on our project teams, how we dispense discipline and who we promote.

Hiring & Promoting

When you open the door to people who are not like you, you avoid sameness within your team. You'll also foster diversity, inclusion, and innovation. Avoiding sameness during hiring means giving equal consideration to qualified candidates who got their academic or technical training at institutions without national name recognition, and being as fascinated by the expertise of those who worked in small companies and start-ups as you are by those who worked for Boeing. Being committed to avoiding implicit bias and actually doing it, however, are two different things.

If Toyota had focused solely on pedigree, I would never have made the cut. When I began working at Toyota as a curriculum developer and a trainer, I was a high school dropout working side-by-side with people that had Bachelor's and Master's and PhDs.

So how can you ask the right questions to help you select the right fit for your team?

- First, clarify what skills and abilities are required for each position on your team. In essence, you are creating the standard for that position. This standard will guide your thought process as you review potential candidates for open positions. It will prevent you from chasing after the wrong candidates. After all, you probably don't want a dog that looks good on a couch — you want one that will take your organization across the finish line.

- Second, assess your current team to determine which skills and abilities are missing. The results of the assessment — when compared to the job description — will give you a good idea about your team's strengths and weaknesses and where you need to fill in the gaps.

- Third, create a series of questions that allows candidates to illustrate proof of those skills and abilities. This will improve your ability to hire people who will thrive in your organization. Questions that ask "How" about recent experiences are a great way to get a snapshot of how a candidate measures up to the skills and abilities you need. For example, you could ask, "Tell me about a recent decision you made that didn't turn out the way you anticipated and *how* you handled it." We all learn from our experiences. Asking questions that highlight a candidate's successes — as well as how they cope with failure — can tell you a lot about future performance.

- Fourth, focus on the person's potential value to your team — not on your implicit biases. During the candidate's responses, wear your metaphorical blinders by asking yourself questions like, "Is the candidate's approach complimentary or a carbon copy of my existing team's approach?" or "Will this candidate help me see ideas and concepts from a different point of view?" or "Does the candidate take the team to a higher level or keep it at status quo?" or "Is this candidate a 'mini me' or do they challenge me by bringing something altogether new in terms of personality, expertise, and viewpoint?" By asking yourself these questions, you can limit the impact of your implicit bias on the selection process.

Another mistake some companies make is using personality surveys as their only or primary method for hiring and promoting; they can be a helpful tool but they aren't all encompassing. Having worked for Toyota Motor Manufacturing in Kentucky (TMMK), I can tell you that one of the reasons they were so successful in such a short period of time was because of their multifaceted hiring process. Great hiring managers need good tools, strong instincts, and practiced skills — like Implicit Bias Blinders.

Building Teams

Left unchecked, our implicit biases can control how we build teams. Think about when you were a child on the playground and had to choose your teammates; you started by picking your closest friends and those you were most familiar with. It wasn't until you ran out of friends that you started to base your selection process on performance. The same thing happens today; the only difference is that the stakes are much higher. Back in the day, you wanted to win but you also didn't want to lose a friend. Today, you have to worry about losing your customers (or even your job and your reputation). Real leaders will sacrifice the comfort of sameness on their teams by seeking out diversity that leads to creativity, innovation, and productivity.

Real leaders will sacrifice the comfort of sameness on their teams by seeking out diversity that leads to creativity, innovation, and productivity.

Dispensing Discipline

When leading, you must treat team members as individuals but you must be consistent in how you apply discipline. Being consistent does not mean you have to treat them exactly the same. An employee with 10 years of perfect attendance with one unexcused/unscheduled absence should not receive the same disciplinary action as a new employee with chronic absenteeism. Likewise, leaders need to be held to a higher standard than their subordinates when looking at similar policy infractions. The key to a successful disciplinary process that limits implicit bias includes clearly written policies and procedures tempered with management discretion. Another valuable tool is a peer evaluation for latter stages of the disciplinary process. At Toyota, when a team member reached the final stages of the disciplinary process, they had the option of pleading their case to a panel of their peers.

Performance Evaluation

Our implicit bias also unfortunately impacts our evaluation of team member performance. When you like a person, it is easier to remember the good things they did. Likewise, if you are not fond of a particular individual, you may find it easier to remember all the things that didn't meet your expectations. Granted, your level of leadership within your organization may limit the impact of your implicit bias in these areas (because, for example, there may be many layers of management between you and the staff, and you might not conduct performance reviews for many people). However, as you move up, there will be a greater chance that your implicit bias can and will impact these areas.

If you refuse to develop a set of implicit bias blinders, the impact of your biases will only increase over time. According to Pew Research, by 2055, the U.S. will no longer have a single ethnic majority.[1] Diversity is a forgone conclusion but inclusion is not. One of my clients has 17 different nationalities working under one roof — not by plan but because of the diverse pool of people they are able to draw from. However, diversity without inclusion (and equity) is a waste of creative potential. Creating a more inclusive culture will produce different perspectives, innovative ideas and help you grow your business in its current space and in new, emerging markets.

Diversity is a forgone conclusion but inclusion is not.

Reflection Question for Lesson 8: List all the ways your team is diverse.

_____

_____

_____

_____

Time for a break! When you're ready, move ahead to another chapter/lesson and then come back to the following START Activity and Passport exercise during your second read-through of the book.

---

1   https://www.pewresearch.org/fact-tank/2016/03/31/10-demographic-trends-that-are-shaping-the-u-s-and-the-world/

START Activity

Put your Implicit Bias Blinders on!

1. Start a conversation about inclusion at your workplace, and include employees at all levels.

2. Seek different views from co-workers across the organization.

3. Embrace diversity in your personal life. Start with food, movies, shopping and holidays. Learn more about how others, as Elizabeth Gilbert famously suggested, "eat, pray and love."

4. Find new places to network. Search for new and interesting groups on Meet Up, LinkedIn or Facebook.

Leadership Education & Application Passport

Part A – *Work with your leadership mentor to complete the Target Outcome and Actions sections below.*

Skill: Selecting the Right Players

Target Outcome: With whom will you be applying your "performance before pedigree" mindset and what are you hoping to accomplish?

_____

_____

_____

_____

Actions: What actions need to be taken before and during the application of this skill?

- _____
- _____
- _____
- _____
- _____

Part B – *With your leadership mentor, review the results of your inclusion efforts. Examine what you took away from this experience and look for ways to continually challenge yourself to operate with an inclusive mindset.*

Results:

- _____
- _____
- _____
- _____
- _____

Takeaways:

- _____
- _____
- _____
- _____
- _____

Once you have completed Parts A and B above, have your leadership mentor initial and date the stamp for this Lesson.

Congratulations! You are one step closer to being the leader you've always dreamed of being.

"The man who promises everything is sure to fulfill nothing, and everyone who promises too much is in danger of using evil means in order to carry out his promises, and is already on the road to perdition."

— *Carl Jung*

LESSON 9

You Have My Word!

Keeping Your Commitments

At one point or another, we've all said or heard the phrase, "You have my word." When someone speaks these words to you, what immediately pops into your head? If you're like me, it varies depending on who said them. Your word is like currency — it can be devalued by the smallest of circumstances.

Your word is like currency — it can be devalued by the smallest of circumstances.

When I was a child, my stepfather would often tell me, "Boy, when you give a person your word, you do it no matter what. In the end, your word is the only thing you have of value." I can still remember the sound of his voice as he said those powerful words. I'd like to think my word is all anyone would ever need from me today but I know that hasn't always been the case.

My first job as an 18-year-old "adult" was as a security alarm monitor for a mom-and-pop security company. My shift was from 6:00 p.m. to 6:00 a.m. I sat in a small narrow room alongside three women who worked an old-fashioned switchboard. (For those of you who have no idea what I'm talking about, Google "Ernestine on Rowan & Martin's Laugh-In.") Now imagine sitting in a corner on a metal folding chair for 12 hours at a time, perched in front of an alarm panel while three operators answered calls and gossiped. That was my world on that very first — very long — night on the job.

After that very long and boring 12-hour shift, I decided I wasn't going back. And I didn't. I ghosted, as we'd say today. A week later, I called my ex-boss and asked to be paid for that one shift. After a few choice words, he told me to meet him at his home. When I got there, he said, "When a man gives me his word, I expect him to follow through. Not only are you not a man of your word, you didn't have the nerve to call me and tell me you wouldn't be back. It took me two hours to find someone to fill that shift and the lady who relieved you almost missed her daughter's Sunday-school play." I was instantly sorry and ashamed. For all my 18 years, I wasn't feeling very "adult" that day.

Since then, I have strived very hard to follow through on my word — by either fulfilling the obligation myself or by making alternate arrangements that were acceptable to the person to whom I had given my word. I know what it feels like when someone breaks their word, and it's problematic not just in the moment but sometimes forever. A broken commitment that lies in the path of a personal or professional relationship makes it more difficult to believe anything that person tells you in the future.

As I'm writing this, my wife and I are overseeing the remodeling of the bathrooms in our house. Our biggest reason for selecting our contractor was that he said he and his partner would do all the work, except for the plumbing and electrical. Not having half a dozen or more contractors traipsing through my house was a big selling point. It was also nice that we would be able to communicate directly with him on a daily basis to make sure everything was moving forward as scheduled. Imagine my surprise when I saw several people from various trades coming and going from my home. I decided to confront Chris, and here's how the exchange unfolded:

Chris: "Well, we have a lot of projects going on now and we can't do the work ourselves."

Me: "Did you know this before we signed the contract?"

Chris: "Yes, but it slipped my mind."

At this point, what do you think his word is worth to me? If you said, "not much!" you'd be correct. A few extra people in my house to ensure a good final result wasn't a horrible price to pay, but I was hung up on the principle. He'd given his word, then invited strangers into my home. You might not be in the midst of a renovation project, but I'm sure you can relate to these moments of miscommunication and broken promises — at work and in life. It takes very little to destroy trust and considerably more to rebuild it.

It takes very little to destroy trust and considerably more to rebuild it.

What are some things you do to make sure your word retains its value?

Being a person of your word means honoring commitments. That's quite easy in the beginning. You see, starting a relationship as a person of your word is easy to do. You do exactly what you say you are going to do. Then life gets in the way and things get complicated. Everyone goes back on their word from time to time, so I'm not suggesting that this is a habit only of "bad people." It's a human habit, and I know we can work to do better.

Let's explore why we sometimes go back on our word. Think about the last time you told someone you'd do something. Why did you say you would? For most of us — in that moment at least — we want to help and it makes us feel good to say *yes*. The problem is that we don't always know what the future will hold. As you can see in the model above, there are two factors that will determine the likelihood that you will keep your word:

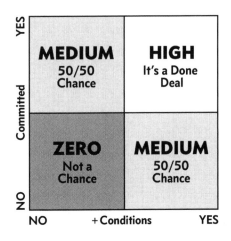

1. Level of commitment

2. Conditions favorable to you as they pertain to each individual situation.

A person will have a high level of commitment if their personal beliefs, values, and motivations are aligned with the promise at the time of execution. In other words, at the time you make the promise, you may have felt one way but your beliefs, values, or motivation may have changed when it came time to execute the promise. The more conditions favorable to you at the time of execution, the greater the chance that you will follow through with the promise. For example, let's imagine that Wednesday evening is the only night during the week you have to yourself. If someone asks for something on that day and you say *yes*, there is a greater chance that you will find a reason for not executing the promise. Your life is already engineered in such a way that you feel exhausted by Wednesday afternoon.

That begs the question: What can you do to increase the likelihood you will keep your word when you give it?

Make fewer promises. If you make 10 promises and only keep three, your word isn't worth much. But if you make three promises and keep all three, your word is golden. The best promise you can make when you are unsure is the promise of consideration. Simply say, "I can't promise you anything right now but give me until the end of the day to think about it and I'll get back to you." This way, you have only committed to getting back to them by the end of the day (or whatever timeframe you establish). Nothing more, nothing less.

Quickly do what you say you're going to do. It's one of the best ways to keep your word. As Benjamin Franklin said, "Don't put off until tomorrow what you can do today." Try to avoid making promises when the execution day is not in the near future. The further the execution date is from the time of making the promise, the greater chance that your life circumstances will change — making it less likely you will follow through. When you postpone unpleasant promises, it increases your stress level. Take your time before responding. Don't promise things you have no desire to do. Don't say *yes* in the moment just because you don't want to let someone down or because you feel bad for them — leader up and say *no*! (There are plenty of ways to do so that are respectful and kind.) If, when you volunteer to do something (or are asked to do something), you know in that moment that it's something you don't want to do and that the promise might not be executable (in terms of the speed, quality, or completeness that is expected), you're apt to eventually find a reason not to keep the promise. By taking your time and thinking it through, you are more likely to promise exactly what you can give. Remember that making promises you don't want to keep (or can't keep) doesn't help anyone; it's far better to disavow the commitment from the get-go.

Don't forget! Another, perhaps obvious, way to increase the likelihood that you'll keep your commitments is to write them down. Even if it's something small, making a note of the promise is important because every promise counts (no matter how big or small). When prioritizing your actions (for the day, week, or month), always rank a promise as a high-priority item to ensure it is one of the first things you do. In addition to reminding yourself about promises and their status, it's important to communicate the status of the promise to the person you owe it to. If you can't deliver on time or in the manner you thought you could, then communicate that as soon as possible. By maintaining open communication, you are showing the other person that you are making an effort to keep your word. In cases in which you have committed to something that is far into the future, increase your communication frequency.

In this modern world, we're often asked to do too much and hold ourselves to impossible standards. We are a culture of "busy-ness" and workaholism, always 10 minutes late to our next appointment and two days behind on our commitments. Culturally, it's become more difficult to say *no* or to do less. But that doesn't mean we can't do better. While it isn't always easy to deliver on your promises, it's crucial that once we give our word, we follow through. I believe it's a hallmark of true leadership and a skill (and attitude) that can be learned.

Like most things, delivering on your promises requires effort. But when you do, you will be seen as responsible, and people will have more trust in you. And if you break a promise, which you will (we all do!), you must apologize; exercise humility and don't let broken promises become a pattern. And because learning to keep your commitments will reduce your stress (your guilt, your fear, your frustration, your anxiety), being a man or woman of your word is as much a gift to yourself as it is to everyone else.

Reflection Question for Lesson 9: What promises did you make today and how many did you (or will you) keep?

_____

_____

_____

_____

Time for a break! When you're ready, move ahead to another chapter/lesson and then come back to the following START Activity and Passport exercise during your second read-through of the book.

START Activity

Keeping your word.

1. Grab a notebook or a blank sheet of paper and write down the promises you've made recently and the specifics surrounding those promises.

2. Identify any barriers that will get in your way of keeping your word.

3. Remove the barriers by shifting other things around or enlisting the help of others.

4. Deliver on your word.

Leadership Education & Application Passport

Part A – *Work with your leadership mentor to complete the Target Outcome and Actions sections below.*

Skill: Keeping your commitments.

Target Outcome: To whom will you be keeping your word and what are you hoping to accomplish by doing so? Why is this important to you?

_____

_____

_____

_____

Actions: What actions need to be taken before and during the application of this skill?

- _____

- _____

- _____

- _____

- _____

Part B – *With your leadership mentor, review the results of your promise-keeping efforts. Examine what you took away from this experience and look for ways to continually be a person of your word.*

Results:

- _____
- _____
- _____
- _____
- _____

Takeaways:

- _____
- _____
- _____
- _____
- _____

Once you have completed Parts A and B above, have your leadership mentor initial and date the stamp for this Lesson.

Congratulations! You are one step closer to being the leader you've always dreamed of being.

"Some people carry their heart in their head and some carry their head in their heart. The trick is to keep them apart yet working together."

— *David Hare*

You're Fired

Making Decisions with Your Circle of Impact in Mind

In a 2017 commercial, Microsoft suggests that we make 35,000 remotely conscious decisions each day (or one decision every two seconds).[1] That sounds like a bit of an exaggeration to me, but who knows? What I do know is that the actions you take at work will ripple out, impacting you, your team, your department, your company, and your customers. In the early years of your leadership journey, the actions you take will be small in comparison to those you will have to take later in your career. Learning to look at how your actions impact your stakeholders is a critical skill — at any stage in your leadership journey.

The other day, I heard someone say, "You should follow your heart when it comes to your passion." What about the rest of the time, like when we're at work, leading people and projects? Should you make decisions with your head or your heart? The decisions you make can have an immediate and lasting impact on your life — as well as your

---

1   https://www.youtube.com/watch?v=6k3_T84z5Ds

company's success. The question is, "How can you make the best decisions for you, the company, and the customer?"

Let's dissect the decision-making process and what goes into it. First, you need to consider your emotional state — as well as your understanding of the issue at hand. Are you in a high or low emotional state? What information do you have and what information are you missing? By taking a moment to inventory your emotional state and the information available, you will be better suited to make decisions.

When I worked for a forklift manufacturer, one of my responsibilities was leading the General Affairs Department, which had responsibility for all the contingent workers (i.e., non-employee temporary contractors). When it came to attendance, the contingent workers were held to the same standard as the full-time team members. While reviewing the daily contingent attendance report, I found that a contingent worker in the Assembly Department had exceeded her acceptable number of absences and needed to be terminated. I went to her supervisor, Brian, to let him know she had pointed out and that he would need to collect the contingent worker's badge and let her know her services were no longer needed. I told Brian he could decide what time was best for him: first break, lunch, second break, or he could even wait until the end of the day. As a supervisor, Brian made decisions every day about where to place his team members for optimal efficiency and productivity. But this was the first time Brian would have to make a decision about the best time of day to terminate a worker.

Ultimately, Brian decided to let her go at first break. The question is: What effect did Brian's decision have on the various circles of impact? To answer that question, we need to take a look at any negative consequences produced by his decision and how far-reaching those negative consequences travel from the center of what I call the circle of impact.

The circle of impact starts with you and ripples outward to the customer. Every action you take will have positive and/or negative consequences. The negative consequences may only have minimal impact or they can have far-reaching impact that ultimately involves the customer. Leaders need to take actions not

just based on what is best for themselves but what is best for the entire circle of impact. Let's take a look at Brian's decision and how it impacted each level of the circle.

The first circle represents the leader. What, if any, negative consequences did Brian suffer as a result of his decision to let the contingent worker go at first break? By letting her go at first break, Brian was left with a process that needed to be covered for the remainder of the shift. Ultimately, Brian pulled his assistant team leader from his training responsibilities to cover the hole. That meant one of Brian's performance objectives — cross-training — would be delayed and filling in the gaps would be more difficult.

The second circle involves the team. If Brian had waited until the end of the day, his team would not have had to work harder to pick up the slack. Because we had an on-site contingent vendor, we had a replacement the next day, minimizing the impact to the team. Additionally, having to cover for the departed contingent worker put the cross-training schedule behind. Both of these consequences can impact morale negatively.

The third circle is the department. In this case, the department made its production target for the day without overtime so there was no appreciable impact.

The fourth level in the "circle of impact" involves the entire company. As it relates to the day and general timeframe of Brian's decision, the company made its shipping target without overtime. Overall, the company was not negatively impacted by Brian's decision. (Other than Brian's manager, who had a meltdown. But that's a story for later in the book.)

And finally, the fifth level of impact involves the customer who, thankfully, did not experience any delay in deliveries or decrease in product or service quality.

Engaging the Head and the Heart in Making Decisions

Now that we know how the impact of Brian's actions rippled outward, let's look at how the head and heart play a part in decision-making. Here are four ways the tug-of-war between your head and your heart can impact your decision-making:

- **Poor Information/Low Emotional State** — When you are in an emotional low, you are more risk averse when it comes to decision-making. Couple that with a lack of viable information and your decision-making fizzles or even shuts down.

- **Good Information/Low Emotional State** — When you have all the information you need to make a well-informed decision and are at an emotional low, you run the risk of taking no action.

- **Poor Information/High Emotional State** — When you are excited and enthusiastic about a situation but lack good intel, it can lead to disastrous consequences. You'll tend to take more risks because your good mood hijacks your thought process.

- **Good Information/High Emotional State** — Like many things in life, the most satisfying outcomes are a result of having balance. The same is true in decision-making. We need a balance between information and emotion for our head and our heart to make the best decisions. We require a thinking process that allows us to select the strongest options with the least negative impact. We also need to consider our emotional state and how it can influence whether or not we take action. The model below shows how the strength of your options and your willingness to act will affect your situation.

Quadrant 1: If you have weak options and don't act, nothing will change. Get input from others to help you find stronger options that you'll be willing to take.

Quadrant 2: If you have strong options in an emotional low, you may be reluctant to act. If you don't act, you are missing an opportunity to make a difference. The key is to focus on the facts surrounding the situation and confirm their validity so you can move forward.

	Strong	Missed Opportunity	Desired Outcome
OPTIONS			
	Weak	Status Quo	Learning Opportunity
		Inaction	Action

Quadrant 3: If you have weak options and act, it's most likely due to an emotional high. Because of the emotional high, you may not realize the options are weak. If you act and your decision fails to get the desired outcome, you need to use it as an opportunity to learn.

Quadrant 4: When the stars align, you have strong options and an emotional high that will allow you to achieve your desired outcome.

Paying attention to your emotions and recognizing how those emotions can hijack your thought process will help create a balance between your head and heart.

Paying attention to your emotions and recognizing how those emotions can hijack your thought process will help create a balance between your head and heart.

I have no proof, but I suspect Brian's decision was more heart than head. I think he didn't want to be seen as a weak leader — he wanted to look decisive, swift, even ruthless. Overall, the decision Brian made did no lasting damage. What we don't know is how the delay in training affected the circle of impact.

None of us makes the perfect decisions. If you procrastinate because you are afraid of making the wrong decision or because you tend to over-analyze the situation, nothing changes. When you're proactive and choose to move ahead, that's when things can change for the better.

Reflection Question for Lesson 10: What decisions did you make today and what part did your head and heart play?

_____

_____

_____

_____

Time for a break! When you're ready, move ahead to another chapter/lesson and then come back to the following START Activity and Passport exercise during your second read-through of the book.

START Activity

___

Check your head and your heart.

Before making your next decision, ask yourself the following questions:

1. What information do you currently have?

2. What information do you need?

3. What is your emotional state?

4. If you make a decision now — with the information you have and in your current emotional state — what negative impacts will there be and how far out will the ripple reach?

Leadership Education & Application Passport

Part A – *Work with your leadership mentor to complete the Target Outcome and Actions sections below.*

Skill: Making Decisions with Your Circle of Impact in Mind

Target Outcome: Who will this decision affect and what are you hoping to accomplish by trying out your new decision-making tools?

_____

_____

_____

_____

Actions: What actions need to be taken before and during the application of this skill?

- _____

- _____

- _____

- _____

- _____

Part B – *With your leadership mentor, review the results of your decision-making efforts. Examine what you took away from this experience and look for ways to always keep your circle of impact in mind when making decisions.*

Results:

- _____

- _____

- _____

- _____

- _____

Takeaways:

- _____

- _____

- _____

- _____

- _____

Once you have completed Parts A and B above, have your leadership mentor initial and date the stamp for this Lesson.

Congratulations! You are one step closer to being the leader you've always dreamed of being.

"Individual grievances and pet peeves have got to go by the wayside. Generally, you don't have to worry about the guys who are playing every day, it's the guys who are sitting on the bench that are the ones that get needles in their pants."

— *Walter Alston*

Makin' Bacon

Understanding the Difference Between Pet Peeves and Performance Issues

One rainy afternoon, my wife, Mart, and I were makin' bacon. I was in the kitchen, doing all the prep work to make one of my famous homemade pizzas. While I was cutting up the veggies, my wife decided to give me a hand and started to microwave the bacon. We both cook it pretty much the same way, with one exception. When I do it, I place a paper towel — diagonally — over the rectangular microwavable bacon tray. This allows me to tuck the four corners under the tray, securing the paper towel in place. My wife, on the other hand, folds the paper towel so that it perfectly covers the tray without hanging over.

"You're doing it wrong," I said when I noticed what she was doing. Then I took the paper towel and placed it over the dish the "Dan way" and said, "That's how you do it." How do you think my wife felt after my know-it-all comment and my insistence on re-doing her work? What do you think she did? Well, without a word she looked at me, turned, and left the kitchen, leaving me to cook the bacon the Dan way.

Looking back, I clearly see that she wasn't doing anything "wrong" at all; I was treating her judgment calls in the kitchen like they were a performance issue when what was really happening was that she had triggered a "pet peeve" for me. Sadly, this happens far too often in the workplace too. For leaders to create strong working relationships, we need to focus on performance issues, not our individual pet peeves. Too often, we let minor annoyances affect how we relate to our spouses, coworkers, clients, friends, and family. If we decide to give someone feedback, we must ensure that we are dealing with performance issues not pet peeves. But how do you know if you are just being picky or performance oriented? When someone is doing something that is irritating you (or doing something differently from the way you might do it), ask yourself one question. It's the question I should have asked myself before opening my mouth. "Is it important?" The key is to determine not whether it's important to *you* but whether it's important in light of six factors that impact your organization's ability to meet the customer expectations. The six factors are: safety, quality, productivity, cost, maintenance, and personnel.

For leaders to create strong working relationships, we need to focus on performance issues, not our individual pet peeves.

Let's take each of these six factors and compare the answers to how my wife folds the paper towel to fit the microwave bacon tray:

- **Safety** — Does my wife's method create a safety hazard? No.

- **Quality** — Does her method produce inferior bacon? No. In fact, it is just as crispy as mine and it tastes just as good as mine.

- **Productivity** — Does folding the paper towel to fit the tray impact the cooking time of the bacon? No. It takes 3 minutes, regardless of how the paper towel is placed on the tray.

- **Cost** — Does it cost more to make the bacon using Mart's method? No. The energy use and number of paper towels is the same.

- **Maintenance** — Does it take longer to clean the microwave when my wife makes the bacon? No. Both methods prevent grease from splattering inside the microwave.

- **Personnel** — Does my wife's method of covering the bacon create any personnel issues? No. It doesn't even bother Quilla (Kee-La) or Tess, our two canine bacon-quality-control inspectors.

If, when examining something that you're harping on your employees about, you can answer *no* to the multifaceted question, "Is it important in light of safety, quality, productivity, cost, maintenance, and personnel?" then you don't have a performance issue — you have a pet peeve.

 Pet Peeves or Performance Issues

Which of the following are pet peeves (PP) or performance issues (PI)? Can some of them be both?

1. Messy workspace	PP	PI
2. Using the floor as a desk	PP	PI

3. Not wearing shoes in the workplace	PP	PI
4. Extreme ornamental piercings	PP	PI
5. Popping chewing gum	PP	PI

If you circled both for all five, you are an A+ student. Each item can be a pet peeve or a performance issue, depending on the environment. If you don't work in a shared workspace, it can't be seen by visitors, your mess doesn't encroach on another person's workspace, or your work habits or adornments don't create a safety hazard, it's not a performance issue. Just because you don't like the way a person does something doesn't mean it's a performance issue. If you can find a valid concern based on one of the six factors (i.e., safety, quality, productivity, cost, maintenance, or personnel), then it is a performance issue that needs to be addressed.

It's been a while since the great makin' bacon fiasco and I have learned not to be so nit-picky and I've also learned to take more time to evaluate a situation before opening my mouth (or repositioning a paper towel). If whatever is getting under your skin, so to speak, doesn't impact safety, quality, cost, productivity, maintenance, or personnel negatively, it's not an issue. When someone's behavior is annoying you but doesn't constitute a performance issue, it can be hard not to say something. In those cases, it is best to remember that if they have behaviors that annoy you, there is a very good chance that you have certain behaviors that are annoying them, too.

The next time you find yourself wanting to express how someone's behavior is annoying you, ask yourself one question: "Is it important?" Is it important in light of safety, quality, cost, productivity, maintenance, or personnel? If it's not, it's a pet peeve — not a performance issue.

And FYI, my wife still does it the wrong way. But I've learned to keep my big mouth shut.

Reflection Question for Lesson 11: What are some things you do that others might find annoying?

_____

_____

_____

_____

Time for a break! When you're ready, move ahead to another chapter/lesson and then come back to the following START Activity and Passport exercise during your second read-through of the book.

START Activity

Is it a pet peeve or a performance issue?

The next time you decide you need to give someone feedback, ask yourself, "Is it important?"

1. What safety issues were created?

2. How was quality compromised?

3. How did the behavior negatively impact productivity?

4. Did the behavior increase cost?

5. Did the behavior create a maintenance issue?

6. How were others impacted negatively?

Leadership Education & Application Passport

Part A – *Work with your leadership mentor to complete the Target Outcome and Actions sections below.*

Skill: Understanding the Difference Between Pet Peeves and Performance Issues

Target Outcome: With whom will you be applying this new way of thinking about workplace annoyances and what are you hoping to accomplish?

_____

_____

_____

_____

Actions: What actions need to be taken before and during the application of this skill?

- _____

- _____

- _____

- _____

- _____

Part B – *Now, take a moment to review the results and what you took away from this experience with your leadership mentor to look for ways to improve your next experience using this skill.*

Results:

- _____
- _____
- _____
- _____
- _____

Takeaways:

- _____
- _____
- _____
- _____
- _____

Once you have completed Parts A and B above, have your leadership mentor initial and date the stamp for this Lesson.

Congratulations! You are one step closer to being the leader you've always dreamed of being.

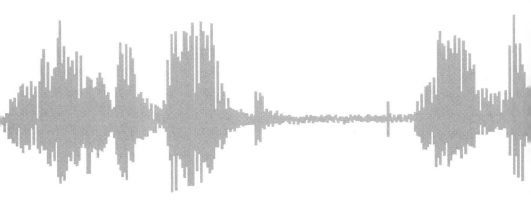

"There is no science in creativity. If you don't give yourself room to fail, you won't innovate."

— *Bob Iger*

Kids and Convicts

Developing Your Team's Creative Muscles

Like many people who grew up in the '60s and '70s, my parents didn't have a lot of disposable income. Going to the movies was something we did once in a blue moon, usually at the drive-in to watch a Disney movie. Those rare times made for some great memories but not my most treasured. Our family had *another* movie tradition that I cherish so much that I've shared it with my children and I still enjoy it to this day.

My step-dad called them "Mr. Moon Movies." On cloudy summer nights, we'd lie on blankets in the backyard, eating homemade popcorn with real butter, drinking Coca-Cola from glass bottles, and gazing at the sky. We each took turns creating our own "movies." The star was always the moon, and bit players were the images our minds conjured up as the clouds glided over the moon. We always laughed and there were never any reruns.

One of the reasons we had so much fun sharing our make-believe Mr. Moon Movies is because there were no wrong answers. Whatever you said was acceptable; it was up to the *others* to try and see your point of view without judging. Your audience had to exercise creativity and follow where you led. This nonjudgmental support and observation are concepts we, as adults, seem to have forgotten. It is so easy to say why something won't work instead of thinking of ways to *make* it work. When we play, we are more open and willing to explore possibilities that don't conform to our mental comfort zones. We need to play more at work.

When we play, we are more open and willing to explore possibilities that don't conform to our mental comfort zones. We need to play more at work.

Losing Our Creative Genius

In his 2011 TEDx talk, "The Failure of Success," Dr. George Land explains how he and Beth Jarman developed a test that would measure creative potential for NASA rocket scientists and engineers.[1] They then decided to study 1,600 children, ages four and five, to see how creative they were. They found that 98% scored at the creative genius level.

Land and Jarman continued to follow that same group, testing their creativity at five-year intervals for 10 years. When the group was tested at age 10, only 30% scored at the creative genius level. By

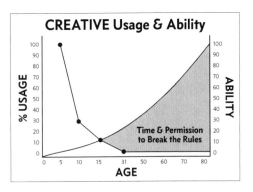

---

1   https://www.youtube.com/watch?time_continue=38&v=ZfKMq-rYtnc&feature=emb_logo

the time the children were 15, only 12% scored at the creative genius level. The researchers decided to jump ahead and give the test to 1 million 31-year-old adults and found that only 2% scored at the creative genius level. It was clear that over time, we're losing our creative genius.

So why are children more likely to be creative while adults aren't? To answer that question, ask yourself what happens to us when we turn 5 or 6? It's simple — we start going to school, where we are taught that there is a right and a wrong answer. We are given rules and structures, and expected to conform. This beats the creativity right out of us.

Now, let's take a look at another group of people: convicts. Most people don't know this, but I've been to prison twice, both times for the same thing — consulting. What I noticed is that convicts are highly creative. They can use everyday items — like toothpaste, facial tissue, and markers — to sculpt chess pieces. Inmate Keith Murphy at the Washington State Penitentiary used cardboard, card-stock drawing paper, paper towels, toilet paper, Q-tips, and floor wax to build realistic miniature models of motorcycles. Inmates are also known to turn everyday items into weapons and tools for self-defense.

So, what do kids and convicts have in common when it comes to creativity? Two things: time and a willingness to break the rules. When my granddaughter, Reagan, was five, she loved to play Chutes and Ladders. I remember an instance when she was four spaces away from a ladder that would allow her to "climb" almost to the game's finish line. She rolled the dice and got upset because she rolled a 5 instead of a 4. She counted out loud as she banged her game piece angrily on the board. When she got to 4, she stopped, looked at me and went up the ladder. I said, "You can't do that." She mustered her best sassy voice and replied, "Yes, I can. I rolled a 5, moved 4, so I have 1 left over for later." It was hard to argue with her logic.

The older we get, the less we use our creative abilities — and this has consequences at work when it comes to problem-solving and innovation. If you want to rev up your team's creativity usage, you need to give them time and permission to break the rules. Here is an activity you can do with your team during your next meeting.

If you want to rev up your team's creativity usage, you need to give them time and permission to break the rules.

Activity: Watch Mr. Moon Movies.

Yeah, I know holding meetings outside on a summer evening is probably not convenient. Instead, have your team take video (using their smartphones) of the moon and clouds, then bring those videos to your next team meeting. Play the videos on a screen and have people take turns sharing their interpretation of the video with the team. Nothing is off limits; nothing is impossible. There are only two rules: first, have fun and laugh, second, throw out all other rules. And don't forget the popcorn!

Mr. Moon Movies aren't just a great way to warm up the creative thinking muscles of your team members; they're also a great way to spend some quality time with your loved ones. The next time there is a cloudy night, grab some popcorn, your favorite drink, and your family, and head outside for some Mr. Moon Movies. You'll create some great memories and maybe a tradition that will be handed down for generations.

It's an organization's ability to think creatively that will allow it to outperform and outlast its competitors. The problem is that most organizations don't make creative thinking a priority. So, flex your creative thinking muscles. Remember that in creative thinking, there are no wrong answers so — Let's hear it!

Reflection Question for Lesson 12: What did you do today to exercise your creativity?

_____

_____

_____

_____

Time for a break! When you're ready, move ahead to another chapter/lesson and then come back to the following START Activity and Passport exercise during your second read-through of the book.

START Activity

_____

Initiate a comedy mash-up with your team.

1. Before your next meeting, give each person on your team a copy of the worksheet on the next page *(available for download at NicerBarkNoBite.com)*.

2. Have them list at least 10 titles/positions they've had.

3. Then, have them list at least 10 hobbies/activities they enjoy.

4. Next, have them fill in the blanks at the bottom of the worksheet by playing around with various combinations until they come up with something funny.

5. Take 10 to 15 minutes at the beginning of your next meeting and have them share their comedy mash-ups.

Asking people to share these in front of you and their peers can be intimidating, so make sure you go first. You need to be willing to be vulnerable if you are going to ask them to be vulnerable. By starting your meeting off with a little play, you'll get everyone in a positive frame of mind, ready to think creatively and generate ideas that may lead to your company's next big innovation.

Comedy Mash-Up Worksheet

🌐 *Also available for download at NicerBarkNoBite.com.*

Dan's example:

I was a cop who liked to fish, which means that If I caught too many fish, I had to write myself a ticket. "ba-dum-bum-CHING"

Example from a workshop:

I was a CPA who liked to cook, which means that I'm very good at cooking the books. "ba-dum-bum-CHING"

Your Turn:

I was a _____ who liked to _____,
         JOB/POSITION   HOBBY/ACTIVITY

which means that _____.
                        MASH-UP RESULT

Leadership Education & Application Passport

Part A – *Work with your leadership mentor to complete the Target Outcome and Actions sections below.*

Skill: Developing Your Team's Creative Muscles

Target Outcome: What are you hoping to accomplish by applying one or more of the creativity suggestions in this lesson?

_____

_____

_____

_____

Actions: What actions need to be taken before and during the application of this skill?

- _____

- _____

- _____

- _____

- _____

Part B – *Now, take a moment to review the results and explore what you took away from this experience with your leadership mentor. Look for ways to improve your next experience in spurring team creativity.*

Results:

* _____

* _____

* _____

* _____

* _____

Takeaways:

* _____

* _____

* _____

* _____

* _____

Once you have completed Parts A and B above, have your leadership mentor initial and date the stamp for this Lesson.

Congratulations! You are one step closer to being the leader you've always dreamed of being.

"We get wise by asking questions, and even if these are not answered, we get wise, for a well-packed question carries its answer on its back as a snail carries its shell."

— *James Stephens*

Just One More Thing

Learning to Teach Rather Than Tell

Have you ever made a mistake at work that had a financial impact equal to or greater than your annual salary? I have. I once had responsibility for five departments, and one of them was Security. Every three years, the Security Guard contract goes out for bid. At the end of the bid process, I selected the best provider based on several criteria — including cost. One year, this process required that we say goodbye to our former security company and onboard a new one. To reduce the potential negative impact of switching from one company to another, I identified a handful of security officers from the old company who I felt did an exceptional job, and I asked the new company to hire them.

A month after the transition, I received a letter from the old security company, which included a bill for $95,000. The letter referenced a no-poaching clause that prohibited hiring their security officers.

I had violated that agreement. In essence, the demand letter from our former security partner said we needed to reimburse them for their recruiting, hiring, and training costs associated with replacing the security officers who we kept after the transition. When I saw that number and read those words, I knew my boss was going to fire me. I imagined a cartoonish character with a beet-red face, steam coming out of his ears, and his combover flapping up and down as he yelled at me.

When I told my boss, Mike, about the bill, I was prepared for the worst. He sat back in his chair, rubbing his chin. When he finally leaned forward, I knew I was toast. Here's how the conversation played out.

> **Mike**: "Why did we go with a different security contractor?"
>
> **Dan**: "They had a better training program and cost 10% less overall."
>
> **Mike**: "Hmm. Dan, what did you learn from this experience?"
>
> **Dan**: "Well, I learned that before I make a decision regarding any contract, I need to read through and understand every aspect of the current contract before taking action."
>
> **Mike**: "Okay, thanks. I appreciate you telling me."

He didn't react anything like I'd imagined. I walked away confused and waiting for the other shoe to drop. Was he going to take care of it or was my next meeting an exit interview with Human Resources? Then, in true Columbo style, he said, "Dan, just one more thing. How often does the security contract go out for bid and will the old company be eligible to bid?" I replied: "Every three years. There were no performance issues. So yeah, they'd be eligible to bid on it again." He then picked up a folder and turned his chair to look out the window. I left, reeling emotionally and thinking about what had just happened.

Instead of reacting emotionally, Mike maintained his composure and responded thoughtfully. Luckily for me I had a positive outcome, I didn't lose my job and I didn't have to pay the security company $95,000. So, what did Mike do that resulted in this positive outcome? He did what great leaders do so well, he became a teacher not a teller. He asked me questions to get me to think about the situation. His questioning got me thinking about what would happen in three years or what would happen if the new company didn't work out.

Ultimately, Mike let me handle the demand letter and its possible fall-out. I called the old security company and set up a meeting with David, my former contact. When David arrived, I ushered him into a meeting room and sat opposite him. I remember sliding the letter across the table toward David, and I could tell he was uncomfortable. I said, "David, you know this wasn't personal. We awarded the contract that was best for our company, financially speaking and in terms of training quality. Your team did a great job, and you didn't lose us over performance. My question to you is this: In three years, when this contract goes out for bid again, do you want to be invited to bid on it? Or, if for some reason this new company doesn't live up to their promises, would you want to be considered to come back?" After a long pause, David slapped his hand down on top of the letter and dragged it toward the edge of the table closest to his body, crumpled up the letter, and tossed it in the recycle bin. I can't remember whether I was holding my breath or if my sigh of relief was audible, but it was surely a memorable moment.

Looking back, I'm grateful that Mike let me solve the problem I had created. It's a leader's job to *teach* — not *tell* — their team members what to do when they bring them a problem. Mike taught me a few key things, then let me go tackle the problem at hand. The next time one of your team members brings you a problem, before you immediately jump right in and solve it for them, consider taking these steps:

- First, get them to relax by asking them a simple question you know they can answer.

- Second, ask them what they've learned from the experience. This shifts their brain into gear by making them reflect on the experience to extract a lesson. Guide them through this examination:

  - "What did you learn from this experience?"

  - "What can you do differently in the future?"

  - "What can you do now to make the situation better?"

- Third, ideally you would like for them to come up with a solution on their own. Start by asking:

  - "What have you done so far?"

  - "How do you plan on handling this situation?"

Asking these questions helps your team member analyze the situation and formulate a solution. If these questions don't result in feasible solutions, you may have to prime the pump further by asking a question that steers him or her in the right direction without telling them the "answer" or how you'd handle it. The last resort is to provide them a specific path to follow. Notice I said provide them with a specific path, not take care of it yourself. Remember, your role is to:

- Hone your team members' critical thinking skills.

- Guide your team members to be proactive and take initiative.

- Build their confidence so they don't have to come to you with every little problem.

Reflection Question for Lesson 13: What opportunities did you take today to teach rather than tell?

_____

_____

_____

_____

Time for a break! When you're ready, move ahead to another chapter/lesson and then come back to the following START Activity and Passport exercise during your second read-through of the book.

START Activity

Teach, don't tell.

The next time someone brings you a problem, guide them with questions to solve the problem themselves.

- Get them to relax by asking them a simple question you know they can answer. Make sure it is relative to the problem.

- Ask them what they've learned from the experience. This shifts their brain into gear by making them reflect on the experience to extract a lesson. Ask them:
    - "What did you learn from this experience?"
    - "What can you do differently in the future?"
    - "What can you do now to make the situation better?"

- Encourage them to come up with solutions.

- If they are having a difficult time and the solution seems obvious to you, you can ask a question that steers them in the right direction without telling them the solution you have in mind.

- If necessary, help them develop a plan of action they can take to solve the problem.

Leadership Education & Application Passport

Part A – *Work with your leadership mentor to complete the Target Outcome and Actions sections below.*

Skill: Learning to Teach Rather Than Tell

Target Outcome: With whom will you be applying this skill and what are you hoping to accomplish?

_____

_____

_____

_____

Actions: What actions need to be taken before and during the application of this skill?

- _____

- _____

- _____

- _____

- _____

Part B – *Now, take a moment with your leadership mentor to review the results and explore what you took away from this experience of teaching rather than telling. Look for ways to improve your next experience in this regard.*

Results:

* _____

* _____

* _____

* _____

* _____

Takeaways:

* _____

* _____

* _____

* _____

* _____

Once you have completed Parts
A and B above, have your leadership
mentor initial and date the stamp for
this Lesson.

*Congratulations! You are one step
closer to being the leader you've
always dreamed of being.*

"One of my greatest talents is recognizing talent in others and giving them the forum to shine."

— *Tory Burch*

Leave Your Business Cards Behind

Creating a Development Playbook

Have you ever made a mistake that turned out *not* to be a mistake after all? Apparent mistakes can sometimes be opportunities in disguise. Take, for example, the following story about running out of business cards. Most people in business have forgotten to replenish their business cards at one time or another. And I suspect it's not something you'd *encourage* someone to do. But after you read this chapter, you might change your mind.

Years ago at Toyota, I was working with a training specialist named Dawn. She and I were hosting a benchmarking meeting with Joe, a training representative from a local engine manufacturer. When everyone arrived, we followed the Japanese custom of introducing ourselves and exchanging business cards. I realized, in that moment, that I had given my last few cards out during a previous meeting and forgot to put more cards in my leather planner. I felt a little embarrassed, so I just walked past everyone and sat in the back of the room.

In my mind, I downplayed the oversight, reminding myself that I was only attending because Dawn invited me — so I could be in the loop and offer input when asked. As far as I was concerned, it was Dawn's show to run. As usual, she did a great job of facilitating the meeting and sharing our training goals, objectives, and programs.

Fast forward two weeks, when Dawn and I were now at Joe's company to learn about their training programs. This time, I made sure to have plenty of business cards to hand out during the introductions. After reading my card, Joe said, "Dan, I'm so sorry! During our last meeting, you just sat in the back of the room observing while Dawn did all the talking. I assumed that you worked for her, not the other way around."

In that brief conversation with Joe, I learned one of my most important lessons as a leader and mentor – *"Help them shine. Leave your cards behind."* It's like Jack Welch, the former CEO of GE, said: "Before you are a leader, success is all about yourself. When you become a leader, success is all about growing others."

Developing Your People, Not "Overseeing" Them

Think about a time when you made a presentation with your boss in the room. When it came time for the question-and-answer period, did the audience look to you or to your boss for answers? When you answered, did they look to your boss for confirmation? If you're accustomed to people deferring to your boss (even after your presentations or on the subject of the projects you lead), you have some idea of what it feels like to be invisible.

Just like a sports coach helps an athlete develop her full potential, leaders must develop their team's full potential. You are responsible for training your team members on relevant skills, analyzing performance, and providing encouragement. Just like a coach, those responsibilities take place before the game, during practice, and on the sidelines between plays. But when the team is on the field in the middle of a play, the coach can't go on the field and fix things. It's the coach's job to let the players perform and shine.

Likewise, in the world of business, the leader — as coach and mentor — must be able to communicate goals and objectives, develop team member skills and abilities, and prepare those employees to take the metaphorical field. Once on the field (or in the meeting, in Dawn's case), the coach needs to remain on the sidelines. When you are on the sidelines, the players can see you in their periphery and know you are there to provide support and guidance if they need you. If you've done your job properly, they will be able to execute the play, adapt to the ever-changing dynamics on the field, and score.

Be careful, however, not to take the sports analogy too far. Unlike athletes on a sports team, your team members at work will not be satisfied playing the same position — game after game. You will not only need to develop their skills in their current position, you'll need to help them develop in a way that helps them achieve their goals and aspirations. This means creating a Team Member Professional Development Plan for each and every member of your team.

It all begins with creating a leadership mentality by trusting your team members and giving them the authority to make certain decisions. Eventually, because you've been giving encouragement from the sidelines where they can see you in their peripheral vision, they will become more and more confident. Start by having each team member set specific goals for their current position, identify other positions of interest and for their promotional aspirations. It will be your job to help them create a playbook for achieving those goals by looking at their experiences and educational needs, and determining how to give them the exposure they need.

🌎 *And be sure to check out NicerBarkNoBite.com for worksheets and other resources you can download to help you in this regard.*

Reflection Question for Lesson 14: How did you let your team members shine today?

_____

_____

_____

_____

 Time for a break! When you're ready, move ahead to another chapter/lesson and then come back to the following START Activity and Passport exercise during your second read-through of the book.

START Activity

Create a playbook for your team members.

First, have each team member begin by stating a professional development goal for each of the three development areas (current position, positions of interest, and promotion interests).

Second, download the Professional Development Plan Matrix that can be found under "book support materials" at NicerBarkNoBite.com.

Third, have each team member reflect on their experience to see how they support the three development areas.

Fourth, help team members define the educational needs for each of the three development areas and the path for acquiring the needed education.

Fifth, identify the areas of exposure each team member will need to enhance their current position, lateral positions, and promotions. There are many simple actions they can take to become more visible:

- Sharing their ideas in meetings.

- Developing their public speaking skills.

- Asking for high-visibility projects.

- Building relationships with people in other departments.

- Sharing their expertise on social media (through professional articles on LinkedIn, etc.).

Leadership Education & Application Passport

Part A – *Work with your leadership mentor to complete the Target Outcome and Actions sections below.*

Skill: Creating a Development Playbook

Target Outcome: With whom will you be applying your new coaching/development skills and what are you hoping to accomplish?

_____

_____

_____

_____

Actions: What actions need to be taken before and during the application of this skill?

- _____
- _____
- _____
- _____
- _____

Part B – *Now, take a moment with your leadership mentor to review the results and explore what you took away from this experience of letting your people shine. Look for ways to improve your ongoing experiences in this regard.*

Results:

- _____

- _____

- _____

- _____

- _____

Takeaways:

- _____

- _____

- _____

- _____

- _____

Once you have completed Parts A and B above, have your leadership mentor initial and date the stamp for this Lesson.

Congratulations! You are one step closer to being the leader you've always dreamed of being.

"I'm going from doing all of the work to having to delegate the work — which is almost harder for me than doing the work myself. I'm a lousy delegator, but I'm learning."

— *Alton Brown*

LESSON 15

Painting a Perfect Picture

Mastering Delegation

For many leaders, delegation is one of the most difficult tasks to master. Why? Because many of us don't want to give up control. Once you learn to give up control and delegate effectively, however, you'll free up your time and your talents so you can focus on other duties and responsibilities that are more appropriate to your leadership level or unique talents.

For many leaders, delegation is one of the most difficult tasks to master. Why? Because many of us don't want to give up control.

Here is a list of task types that you should consider delegating:

- Routine tasks
- Interesting tasks

- Tasks others could do better

- Tasks others might enjoy

- Tasks good for development

- Time-consuming tasks

- Tasks for which you're not responsible.

Four Levels of Delegation

There are four basic delegation levels. To illustrate the four levels, let's say you want someone to paint a picture of a sunset where the sun looks like it is just kissing a body of water. At level one, the delegator makes all the decisions and provides the team member with step-by-step instructions that they carry out in order to complete the task. In essence, you are handing the team member a paint-by-numbers task. All the details — like the type and colors of paint to be used, background, foreground, perspective, and all other details — have been decided in advance. The painter just needs to paint exactly what you've outlined.

At level two, the team member makes the decisions but only after consulting with the leader. The team member creates a sketch of the perfect sunset based on the criteria given to them by the leader. The leader then provides feedback on the sketch so the team member can make adjustments to the final product.

At level three, the team member makes all the decisions and doesn't have to check in with the leader until the end of the project. The leader is basically saying, "Draw the sketch and color it in, frame it, hang it on the wall, and let me know when you are done."

At level four, the highest level of delegation, the leader says, "Paint me a sunset where the sun is kissing a body of water" ... then hands the team member a brush and walks away. When you delegate at this level — describing the deliverable but not the process — you are trusting your team member's skills and abilities to complete the project without interference. As long as the criteria of "a sunset kissing a body of water" is met, you are okay with the result — and whatever process was used to create the painting. The sun could be kissing the ocean, a pond, a creek running through a pasture, or even a mirage in the middle of a barren desert. It doesn't matter, as long as the basic criteria and deadline are met.

Planning for Successful Delegation

When you are considering delegation, you need to look at all the tasks that are occupying your time and talents to identify those you can and should let go of, particularly those tasks that will provide development opportunities for your team members. Next, consider the skills and abilities of your team members to determine which tasks to delegate to whom.

When you are considering delegation, you need to look at all the tasks that are occupying your time and talents to identify those you can and should let go of, particularly those tasks that will provide development opportunities for your team members.

Create or customize a "delegation planning form," which can be downloaded at NicerBarkNoBite.com. List all the tasks that are wasting your time and talents on the left side of the form. At the top, write in the names of each of your team members. Fill in the pie chart for each person's skill level and abilities for each task.

Now, review the form to identify any tasks that do not have anyone at a level four (i.e., for which you don't have anyone who could easily take the assignment and run with it, without detailed instruction or supervision). Once you've identified any holes in the matrix, select someone on your team to be trained or leveled up in that area. Write their name on the right side of the matrix across from the specific task. Make sure you designate someone to train that person and set a target date for completion.

This type of planning creates major opportunity for your team, your overall organization, and for you. The next time you need to delegate a task, you'll have all the information you need to delegate like a pro.

Handing Off the Work

Of course, knowing what tasks need to be delegated and who to delegate the tasks to is only part of your responsibility. Now you actually have to delegate the task.

First, be clear about the task you'd like your team member to complete. Describe the goal and specific outcome you will be looking for at the completion of the task. Be specific and communicate when the task needs to be completed.

Second, determine what level of delegation you will be giving the team member. Letting someone else complete a task for you requires a great deal of trust on your end. Because it requires trust, you might be tempted only to delegate tasks to those on your team with a level-four delegation ability. I definitely understand that, but your primary job as a leader is to develop your team members so *they* can learn, grow, and improve.

Third, ask questions to ensure your team members understand exactly what needs to be done and how much freedom they are being afforded to do so. Most mistakes are due to misunderstandings — not knowing exactly what the goals and outcomes are for the task.

Fourth, follow up to ensure that people are on task. During the initial conversation, set checkpoints so you can see how things are progressing. This is especially important when delegating to a level one or two. Touching base with team members at various points along the way is not just for your peace of mind but to provide help and support they are likely to appreciate. Indeed, you never know when someone will be too embarrassed to check in on their own but might feel grateful for a few minutes of your perspective and help. If you wait until the last minute to check in, you're leaving a lot to chance — for you, for them and for your organization.

Fifth and finally, provide feedback as necessary — especially if your team members are working on a task they've never done before. Coaching is a critical aspect of the delegation process. It is essential for removing barriers and ensuring an ideal outcome.

Coaching is a critical aspect of the delegation process. It is essential for removing barriers and ensuring an ideal outcome.

Reflection Question for Lesson 15: What items did you delegate today and what level of delegation did you give? If you didn't delegate, what could you have delegated or what can be delegated in the coming days?

Time for a break! When you're ready, move ahead to another chapter/lesson and then come back to the following START Activity and Passport exercise during your second read-through of the book.

START Activity

Create a delegation development form.

(Follow the instructions below and consider downloading the form template at NicerBarkNoBite.com.)

1. Identify tasks you can delegate using the bulleted list of categories on the first page of this chapter.

2. Write those tasks on the left side of the delegation development form.

3. List your team members' names at the top of the form.

4. Fill in the pie charts based on each person's ability to perform each task.

5. Review the form to see where you need to develop more skill.

6. Based on your team members' strengths and weaknesses, pair people together to train each other up.

7. Start delegating.

Leadership Education & Application Passport

Part A – *Work with your leadership mentor to complete the Target Outcome and Actions sections below.*

Skill: Mastering Delegation

Target Outcome: With whom will you be applying your new delegation skills and what are you hoping to accomplish?

_____

_____

_____

_____

Actions: What actions need to be taken before and during the application of this skill?

- _____

- _____

- _____

- _____

- _____

Part B – *Now, take a moment with your leadership mentor to review the results and explore what you took away from this experience of delegating more effectively and proactively. Look for ways to improve your ongoing experiences in this regard.*

Results:

- _____

- _____

- _____

- _____

- _____

Takeaways:

- _____

- _____

- _____

- _____

- _____

Once you have completed Parts A and B above, have your leadership mentor initial and date the stamp for this Lesson.

Congratulations! You are one step closer to being the leader you've always dreamed of being.

Initials: _____
Date: _____

"So, when you are listening to somebody, completely, attentively, then you are listening not only to the words, but also to the feeling of what is being conveyed, to the whole of it, not part of it."

— *Jiddu Krishnamurti*

Make It Smaller

Redefining "Listening"

If you can hear without listening, can you listen without hearing? And do you really hear what you *think* you hear or just what you *want* to hear? The answer is ... "It depends."

There is perhaps no greater skill for a business leader than that of being a good listener, so it surely warrants our attention in this book and every day in our real lives. How do you define "listening?" Most people think listening is done with your ears. The fact is that listening is a cognitive function. Listening combines the auditory system (outer, middle and inner ear), eyes and the brain. The auditory system collects sound and transforms it into electrical impulses that the brain can interpret. At the same time, the eyes are collecting nonverbal clues and cues that the brain uses to help make sense of what it is hearing.

The problem is that the brain is lazy and likes to take shortcuts; it will take the path of least resistance if you don't hold it accountable. A perfect example comes from a 1950s TV show called *Dragnet.* It was before my time, but I watched the reruns. All my life — and for most others who watched the show — we remember hearing the lead character say (on many occasions), "Just the facts, ma'am." The truth is that it never happened. I never heard him utter those words and neither did you. But we did hear other people say those words. They didn't get it from the show either. They actually got it from listening to a Capitol Records audio satire that spoofed *Dragnet*. It was a 45-rpm single with two recordings — one called "Little Blue Riding Hood" and the other called "St. George and the Dragnet." In the second of the two parodies, the detective, St. George, repeatedly said, "I just want to get the facts, ma'am." But over time, the general public remembered just four of the eight words (i.e., "Just the facts, ma'am" vs. "I just want to get the facts, ma'am") and were sure they heard it on the original *Dragnet* television show, not on a two-sided record featuring comedian Stan Freberg.

This pop culture example is a reminder that we need to pay closer attention to what we hear and what it really means. In the workplace, making a *Dragnet*-style mistake (like attributing the wrong words to the wrong colleague) could be catastrophic. To understand the true messages you're receiving at work, you need to follow a process. I call this "REAL Listening." REAL Listening is the process of thinking about what we hear and see as it relates to our experiences. Every piece of data that our senses provide to our brain passes through our experiential filter.

This past summer, I witnessed a husband and wife across the street as they were engaged in a discussion. Even though I could not hear a single word they were saying, I turned to my wife and said, "I'll bet they are getting a divorce."

Sure, enough within the next two weeks, the wife moved out and the husband's girlfriend moved in. Unfortunately, I had predicted this sad outcome based initially on their body language. The data received by my brain through my eyes — coupled with my previous experiences as they relate to broken and angry hearts — allowed me to understand the message without hearing their words.

So yes, you can listen without hearing. Their body language spoke just as clearly to me, as if I'd been standing next to them.

I blame the dictionary for our misconceptions about listening. Consult any dictionary and you'll see definitions like these:

- To give attention with the ear; attend closely for the purpose of hearing

- To pay attention; heed; obey

- To wait attentively for a sound.

Not one of these three descriptions gets to the heart of REAL Listening. REAL Listening is about understanding. In order to understand, we need to do more than hear sound, pay attention or wait attentively.

Hearing the words and seeing body language can improve your accuracy. However, it takes more than hearing and seeing to be an effective listener. It requires you to get REAL! Yes, you guessed it — REAL is another one of my acronyms. REAL Listening is the process of moving from passively hearing the words to actively:

Reflecting | Engaging | Analyzing | Letting Go!

REAL Listening – Reflection

Reflection is the first part of the listening process. During a normal conversation, your ears and eyes collect data in the form of words, tone of voice, body language and facial expressions. However, reflection doesn't begin until you make a conscious decision to think about that data.

Up to that point, your ears and eyes were just performing their biological function: data collection. When you consciously decide to understand, that is when the listening process begins. As you consciously reflect on the data provided by your ears and eyes, a message (or even an entire story) begins to materialize. This message can — and most likely will — be biased by your experiential filter. Not to worry! At this point, your interpretation of the message is just a baseline. This baseline is explored further during the remaining steps in the process.

REAL Listening – Engagement

During the second part of the listening process, you engage with the speaker to clarify whether your interpretation of the message is accurate. This is done by questioning and paraphrasing — not "parrot phrasing." As you might have guessed, parrot phrasing is just repeating the speaker's words back to them.

Questioning allows you to get clarification on details, while para-phrasing allows you to express your interpretation of the speak-er's words. There are two benefits to sharing your interpretation with the speaker. First, the speaker is able to provide you feedback on your interpretation. The second benefit results from the paraphrasing and validation process between the listener and the speaker, which nearly always triggers a deeper conversation that unearths additional meaning and new opportunity.

Have you ever had a hard time expressing an idea? It happens to most of us. Sometimes we just need to talk our way through our own ideas. As the listener and speaker volley back and forth in this game of verbal tennis, the speaker and the listener are able to gain greater clarity about the situation. If the speaker is not completely clear, it will be hard for you as the listener to provide the necessary support. In essence, as a REAL listener, you are coaching the speaker to a higher level of understanding, which may lead them to make better decisions and solve their own problems. Let's face it — we would much rather come up with our own solutions than have someone tell us what to do. And great coaches and "REAL" listeners can help guide us to our own solutions.

REAL Listening – Analysis

The engagement and analysis process work hand-in-hand. During the engagement process, you will also be conducting an analysis of the verbal and non-verbal data flowing through your experiential filter. This is done in order to identify any inconsistency or hidden meaning within the words. When you detect an inconsistency, you can ask a question or paraphrase to gain clarity. In addition to inconsistencies between facts and statements, there may be an inconsistency between a specific word or phrase and the intended emotion related to the word or phrase.

Asking a clarifying question can be a game changer. During a recent conversation, a friend relayed to me how a single question had kept him from wasting tens or even hundreds of hours writing the wrong book. He participates in a "mastermind" networking group, where he talked about his passion and asked the group for ideas on what his next steps should be. One member suggested that he write a book, and the idea was met with great enthusiasm by everyone. He started talking about what the book would be about and everyone provided encouragement and told him it was a great idea. Well, almost everyone. There was only one problem. The book he was describing had nothing to do with his passion. Instead of the book focusing on his passion, it was about how to run a "lunch-and-learn program." When he was asked, "What does running a lunch-and-learn have to do with your passion?" He said, "Nothing. But it's a book I can write in my sleep."

Asking a clarifying question can be a game changer.

Everyone was "hearing" him talk about writing a book; no one was "listening" to what the book ought to be about. Once the question was asked, everyone changed course and started saying, "No, you need to write a book about your *passion* if that's what you want to speak about from the stage." Had a clarifying question not been asked, this fledgling business author would be locked away right now writing a book that has nothing to do with his passion. Questions help us analyze the situation, gain clarity and lead to better understanding on both sides.

REAL Listening – Let Go!

"Let Go" — the fourth part of the REAL Listening process — is probably the most difficult. In the 2013 movie, *Man of Steel*, there is a scene where a school-age Clark Kent becomes overwhelmed by sensory input from his ears and eyes. He runs out of the classroom and hides in a closet, hoping to escape the sensory overload. But it doesn't work. When his mom shows up, he tells her, "The world is too big, Mom." She replies, "Then make it small."

How can we, as leaders, make the world small — more focused, intentional and intimate? If we want to be REAL Listeners, we need to "make it small" by focusing our attention on the audible and visual data being projected by the messenger. That means we must "Let Go" of:

- Our need to control the conversation

- Our impulse to interrupt

- Our need to share our opinions

- Our habit of jumping in to solve the person's problems

- Our judgements

- Our need to finish someone's sentence

- Our tendency to tell the person what to do.

If our brain is focused on all our needs as we try to listen, we will be like young Clark Kent. Our brain will be overloaded and we will be better off sitting in a closet, trying to shut it all out. This is not to say that you should never share your opinions or solutions — dialogue is eventually vital. But the trick is to wait until you are sure there is a common understanding shared by you and the speaker. Even then, you should still wait to offer your take until after you've been asked. If you're not asked, you can always say, "May I offer some suggestions or give you my initial thoughts?"

Poor listening skills can lead to many problems, including:

- Botched assignments

- Unhappy customers

- Missed targets

- Poor morale

- Unsolved problems

- Failed personal and professional relationships

- Accidents or even death.

Imagine how much time, money and human life could be saved if we could find a way to improve our ability to understand. Understanding comes through REAL Listening. It requires time, resolve, energy and focus.

Understanding comes through REAL Listening. It requires time, resolve, energy and focus.

Remember, hearing is a biological function made possible by your ears. Listening is a thinking process made possible by shifting your brain from a passive state to an active state.

Reflection Question for Lesson 16: Think about the conversations you had today. What were some of the distractions that interrupted your listening?

 Time for a break! When you're ready, move ahead to another chapter/lesson and then come back to the following START Activity and Passport exercise during your second read-through of the book.

START Activity

Practice REAL listening.

1. Have a short conversation — once a day for a week — with a different co-worker each day. Make a concerted effort to follow the REAL Listening method.

2. So you don't get distracted by trying to remember the process ... Focus on the "R" on the first day, the "E" on the second day, the "A" on the third day, the "L" on the fourth day and all four parts on the fifth day.

3. After each conversation, take time to reflect on how well you did.

Leadership Education & Application Passport

Part A – *Work with your leadership mentor to complete the Target Outcome and Actions sections below.*

Skill: Redefining "Listening"

Target Outcome: With whom will you be applying this skill and what are you hoping to accomplish?

_____

_____

_____

_____

Actions: What actions need to be taken before and during the application of this skill?

- _____
- _____
- _____
- _____
- _____

Part B – *Now, take a moment with your leadership mentor to review the results and explore what you took away from this experience of "REAL Listening." Look for ways to improve your ongoing experiences in this regard.*

Results:

- _____

- _____

- _____

- _____

- _____

Takeaways:

- _____

- _____

- _____

- _____

- _____

Once you have completed Parts A and B above, have your leadership mentor initial and date the stamp for this Lesson.

Congratulations! You are one step closer to being the leader you've always dreamed of being.

"The most important thing people did for me was to expose me to new things."

— *Temple Grandin*

Feed Your Brain

Expanding Your Creativity

When it comes to the way you lead at work, are you cultivating critical thinking or conformity? My granddaughter, Reagan, has been known to fracture a rule or two when playing board games — conformity is not her strong suit. Although she is generally looking out for her own best interests (i.e., is a bit selfish, though sassy and lovable), she usually has a sound explanation that's hard to argue against.

My daughter, Jeannie, called me first thing in the morning to tell me how Reagan used her critical thinking skills at school. You see, Reagan got a wrong answer on a true/false test and didn't understand why the teacher wouldn't accept her answer. The question was: "The easiest and cheapest type of communication is always running to the person you want to speak with and talking face-to-face." TRUE/ FALSE? The answer the teacher was looking for was "TRUE." Reagan, on the other hand, took the question literally and applied it to the relationships in her life. Reagan answered "FALSE." (False, by the way, is the correct answer — not that I'm biased in any way.)

When Reagan received her test with the answer marked wrong, she asked the teacher why. The teacher explained, "It is always easier and cheaper to talk to people face-to-face." That response really didn't answer the question; it was like saying, "Because I said so." Reagan replied, "Well, I'd have to have my mom drive me to Kentucky every time I wanted to talk to my O'pa. I think talking to him on the phone would be easier and cheaper except for when he comes to visit." *That's my girl!!!*

I know the teacher was trying to get her students to see that face-to-face communication is usually the most *effective* form of communication. However, that is not what she asked.

The teacher was more interested in getting *her* answer to the question than cultivating critical thinking. I'm both proud and sad that my granddaughter was the only one in her class to get the answer wrong. I'm proud because she has been taught by her parents to think and reason. I'm sad because the other children are just learning to conform to the "right" (or popular or expected) answer instead of learning to think and reason.

Creative Thinking in the Workplace

Have you ever had an "AHA! Moment" — you know, where an idea or solution pops into your head, seemingly out of nowhere? In the LinkedIn Learning 2020 Workplace Learning Report,[1] creative thinking was identified as the number one soft skill companies need. To help their companies not only meet but exceed the expectations of customers, leaders need to develop a more creative mindset for themselves and their team members.

---

1   https://learning.linkedin.com/resources/workplace-learning-report

To help their companies not only meet but exceed the expectations of customers, leaders need to develop a more creative mindset for themselves and their team members.

"Think outside the box!" It's a common suggestion, and I'm guessing you remember someone saying it to you at some point. You may even have said those words to someone else. The problem is that it's impossible to think outside the box. The box is your brain and it's the only place you know how to "think." The only creative thinking resource we have available to use at any given moment is drawn from the collective knowledge and experiences we've accumulated over time.

Think of the brain as a box with many other small boxes inside of it. Each box is a specific type of knowledge or an experience you've had. Creativity and innovation come when you dump out the contents of those boxes and mix them up. The more boxes you have in your brain, the more resources you have available for creative and critical thinking. Creativity requires an active, present, focused brain. A creative brain is one that has a thirst for new knowledge and is hungry for new experiences. The question is, "How do you increase your ability to be creative and the ability of your team members?" It's simple. You have to feed your brain with nutrients that will nourish creativity. There are numerous ways to fuel the brain's creative abilities. My three favorites are reading, having new experiences, and asking stupid questions.

How can *you* get started with fueling your creativity? Read daily from a *physical* book (i.e., a paperback or hard cover book, not just an eBook) for 10 to 15 minutes a day. Don't just read it — underline, highlight and dogear it. The act of reading and interacting with the book in a physical way helps you retain the information you read. And retention is important because the more you retain, the more creative nutrients you have available to you the next time you need to think innovatively or in a fresh way. Read books that are outside of your normal interests. Reading about subjects you are already familiar with doesn't boost your creativity. To get your creative juices flowing, start devouring books you wouldn't normally read, like books recommended by friends who are very different from you. You can also read magazines, cookbooks, poetry, comic books, or any other form of text that falls outside of your normal reading.

Creativity and imagination are fueled by learning. Your willingness to learn about new subjects increases your ability to imagine and be creative. Notice that I said "learn about" — not "become an expert in." The idea is to become versed in many subjects and, therefore, a fascinating conversationalist at cocktail parties. And knowing a little bit about everything gives you a treasure trove of ideas and insights to draw from when thinking at and about work.

Aside from reading, the best experience is, in fact, an *experience*. Try something new, knowing that getting out of your comfort zone forces your brain to adapt and to create new memories. These new memories become fuel for creativity. In my case, I've tried every-thing from triathlons to riding bulls, from jumping out of airplanes to being electrocuted during Tough Mudder obstacle-course races. I don't just do these activities for the adrenaline rush, it's not for the bruises, and it's definitely not for the mud in my shorts. It's finishing and learning from these experiences that drives me to get outside my comfort zone. Open your mind to new and unexplored paths. Coming up with creative ideas is challenging and sometimes fright-ening. But the new experience itself doesn't have to be frightening or even adrenaline-producing. I've been the human bait for guard dog training but I also love growing bonsai trees and traveling to new destinations. Do what appeals to you and piques your curiosity. Don't be afraid to try something new. When you keep doing the same things, you will keep getting the same results. Challenging yourself to experience new adventures will help you get better results when it comes to being creative.

Our brain is lazy and likes routines. If you're like most people, you spend most of the time going to the same restaurants, eating the same food, hanging out with the same group of people, and listening to the same genre of music. Trying something new can improve your creative thinking skills. For me, that means swapping that big fat juicy bacon cheeseburger for a plate of sushi. I can compound the impact of that experience by eating that sushi at a real Japanese restaurant and learning about Japanese culture and cuisine.

Creativity comes about by asking so-called stupid questions and having the courage to answer them — just as we explored in Lesson 7, Seeing with Four Sights, Not Four Eyes, when we looked at how Uber and Airbnb found a new and innovative way to look at their businesses. Odd, stupid, highly irregular questions that challenge your assumptions do something remarkable — they engage your brain, making it possible to solve problems you've never considered before. Even the most creative people can benefit from feeding their brain with new information and experiences.

Odd, stupid, highly irregular questions that challenge your assumptions do something remarkable — they engage your brain, making it possible to solve problems you've never considered before.

Reflection Question for Lesson 17: What was the last book you read? What food did you recently eat that was out of your norm? What was the last activity you participated in?

 Time for a break! When you're ready, move ahead to another chapter/lesson and then come back to the following START Activity and Passport exercise during your second read-through of the book.

START Activity

___

Feed your brain to expand your creativity.

1. Think of three subjects that are of interest to you, buy or borrow one book on each, and then read them.

2. Go to a restaurant that serves food you wouldn't normally eat, and give it a try.

3. Make a list of things you've always thought would be fun to do but are outside of your comfort zone. Do some research on them and then pick one and do it.

4. Keep a stupid question journal. Take time once a week to ask a stupid question and write down all your ideas without judgement.

5. Get your team involved. Have an ethnic mash-up lunch where everyone brings a dish from a different cultural tradition.

Leadership Education & Application Passport

Part A – *Work with your leadership mentor to complete the Target Outcome and Actions sections below.*

Skill: Expanding Your Creativity

Target Outcome: With whom will you be applying this skill and what are you hoping to accomplish?

_____

_____

_____

_____

Actions: What actions need to be taken before and during the application of this skill?

- _____

- _____

- _____

- _____

- _____

Part B – *Now, take a moment with your leadership mentor to review the results and explore what you took away from this experience of feeding your brain to trigger better creativity. Look for ways to improve your ongoing experiences in this regard.*

Results:

- _____
- _____
- _____
- _____
- _____

Takeaways:

- _____
- _____
- _____
- _____
- _____

Once you have completed Parts A and B above, have your leadership mentor initial and date the stamp for this Lesson.

Congratulations! You are one step closer to being the leader you've always dreamed of being.

"Whenever you're in conflict with someone, there is one factor that can make the difference between damaging your relationship and deepening it. That factor is attitude."

— *William James*

Stop, Drop, and Roll

Maintaining Professionalism Under Pressure

Do you remember the old saying we had as children, "Sticks and stones will break my bones, but words will never hurt me?" Even though most of us have said it countless times, we know the pain from judgmental or hate-filled words can last far longer than the pain of a broken bone. The other day, I got a really snarky and rude email from an acquaintance — a person who I can only describe as barely being a blip on the outer edges of my social radar. Even though his words should mean absolutely nothing to me, the email still made my blood boil. I actually had little beads of sweat forming on my forehead as I read it.

As we know from reading Facebook posts and Twitter comments, there are two ways people typically handle these situations. Some people will respond with venom in the heat of the moment, escalating the situation and fueling the fire. Others will sit and stew about the remarks, making it hard for them to focus on anything else. The first approach may make us feel better in the moment but can easily destroy any relationship we have or hope to have with that person. The second increases the stress and frustration we feel personally, which ends up affecting our work and health.

When was the last time someone said or did something that made your blood boil? How did you handle it? If I had received this same email when I was in my 20s, I would have not only rubbed my acquaintance's metaphorical nose it, I would have rubbed his whole face in it. Thankfully, I learned a new way — a way that is more about compassion than power.

I think my friend and fellow speaker Doug Semenick says it best with his "50% Rule." It states, "50% of what I am getting ready to say is true to me, but if I say it to this person, at this time, in this situation, it won't be helpful." It won't be helpful to the other person and it won't ultimately help you.

In Lesson 10, I introduced you to Brian, the Assembly supervisor who needed to terminate one of his contingent workers for poor attendance. As Paul Harvey would say, this is the rest of the story. Later that day, I was walking from my desk in our open office to the copy room. Halfway to my destination, I was confronted by Dean, the Assembly assistant manager, who started yelling, "Who the hell do you think you are? Why the hell did you fire that woman at first break instead of waiting until the end of the day? Are you some kind of idiot?"

When someone sends you an email that sets you off, you have the ability to decompress before you respond so you don't react in the heat of the moment. But what do you do when the conflict is literally "in your face?" Dean was in my space and "all bowed up," looking for a fight. I really thought he might throw a punch; he was clearly very angry. So, that begs the question: "How do we, as leaders, deal with such a situation in a way that allows for emotional closure while maintaining our professional demeanor and the relationship?

It's simple.

STOP — DROP — ROLL

The next time you are in a face-to-face conflict, try these three steps:

STOP

Stop your emotions from hijacking your mouth. Remain calm. If you respond in kind, you will only escalate the situation. The most important thing you can do when dealing with someone who is being aggressive toward you is to maintain your composure. You've probably heard the flight attendant announcement about oxygen masks: "In case of emergency, oxygen masks will drop down in front of you. Please pull the mask down toward your face and place the mask over your mouth and nose. If you are traveling with a child, please put your mask on first, then attend to the child. Breathe in normally and adjust the face straps like this."

The most important thing you can do when dealing with someone who is being aggressive toward you is to maintain your composure.

The same is true when it comes to close-quarter conflict. You need to take measures to ensure *you* can breathe before attending to the child. When you take a deep breath, it triggers the parasympathetic nervous system, calming you down. It regulates the hormones coursing through your body, making it easier for you to respond in an appropriate manner. Reacting in the heat of the moment can turn a manageable dispute into a war of wills that escalates exponentially. By stopping, rather than reacting, emotionally intelligent leaders create space to consider the situation from all angles and can choose the best approach for handling the situation.

DROP Back

Physically and figuratively drop back a step. In my martial arts and workplace violence avoidance class, I teach my students what I call the "Natural Stance." At the onset of the aggressive behavior, let your dominant leg drop back, reducing your frontal exposure. Cross your arms and then take the arm closest to your aggressor and pivot at the elbow, letting your hand rest on your chin as though you were assuming the "Thinker" pose. Now nod your head as though you are contemplating what they are saying. This stance provides you the opportunity to react to any physical aggression and makes you look non-threating and thoughtful. Granted, 99.9% of the conflicts you encounter will not leave you feeling physically threatened, but knowing this simple technique can help defuse the situation and might come in handy on the streets. If you happen to be seated during a conflict, drop back in your chair away from the person and maintain an open and relaxed posture. Nod your head, say "mm-hmm," as a sign you are paying attention.

The second way for you to drop back is to establish some ground rules for continuing the discussion. Don't interrupt the aggressor, as this will likely cause them to escalate. Once they run out of steam or pause for a breath, say something like, "If you want to continue this discussion, I need you to stop raising your voice and cursing at me." Dropping back physically and figuratively while stopping your emotions from hijacking your mouth, will keep you safe and keep the conflict from escalating. Now it's time for you to apply the third part of the formula.

ROLL

Ready for another acronym? Great! The final part of maintaining your professionalism under pressure involves what I call "ROLL" — reflect on what you heard, open a dialogue, leave the conflict gracefully, and then let it go.

Reflect on what you heard them say. Are they upset with you, the situation or something else? Once you think you are sure about what is causing the aggression, use your paraphrasing skills to feed your interpretation back to them. This may be the most difficult part, because our natural response is to hit back when we've been attacked. But you've just taken a breath and dropped back, so you're collecting yourself. Now say something like, "I can see how losing six hours of productivity would be frustrating."

Open a dialogue so you can share your side of the story. To keep the person from feeling attacked, use "we"-focused language in favor of "you"-focused language. This will show the other person you are dedicated to addressing the problem, not scrutinizing the person. Conflict requires at least two people, so it will take all parties working together to move forward. Share something you can do to prevent the problem from happening again. Then ask the other person what could be done from their side to prevent the issue from happening again. Find common ground.

Leave the conflict gracefully once you and the other person come to an understanding. Move on and don't look back. You only have to *work* with the person; you don't have to be their best friend.

Let it go! Don't let the conflict fester into a grudge. Move on, maintaining a professional demeanor and letting bygones be bygones. At the end of any conflict or after firing someone, my goal was always to get them to shake my hand (but never to force them into doing it). There is something called the "Male Warrior Hypothesis," which suggests that men shake hands after conflict to ensure they can call on them for help in the future.

And there you have it — Stop, Drop, and ROLL.

Let's return for a moment to that fateful day when Brian had to let a contingent worker go, and Dean let me have a piece of his mind. While Dean was cursing me out, I noticed Brian standing behind Dean, trying to hide his 6'4"-tall 250-pound self behind Dean's 5'10", 175-pound stature. I was not about to get sucked into an altercation that was about Brian's decision, which I trusted him to make. So, I turned to Brian and said: "Brian, what did you tell me when I asked you if you wanted to wait until the end of the shift to terminate her?"

Brian replied with a simple: "No."

With Dean still standing between us, I asked Brian: "When I asked if you wanted to let her go at lunch, what did you say?"

Brian again promptly responded: "No, if we have to let her go, send her home at first break."

I'm sure you can guess what happened next. Dean turned on Brian like a starving piranha after a side of beef. You know what they say, "It takes two to tangle." Okay, so it's tango — but in this case, tangle is more appropriate.

When aggression or conflict bursts wide open in your face, maintain a cool, calm head. If you do, you will be able to keep the situation from escalating and hopefully keep from getting punched in the nose. Being a leader often requires a high level of composure and professionalism. The next time someone makes your blood boil, Stop, Drop, and Roll.

Reflection Question for Lesson 18: What was the last thing someone did to make your blood boil and how did you react?

_____

_____

_____

_____

Time for a break! When you're ready, move ahead to another chapter/lesson and then come back to the following START Activity and Passport exercise during your second read-through of the book.

START Activity

Practice the "Stop — Drop — Roll" method.

Most of us don't encounter conflict on a regular basis but there are a couple of techniques you can practice every day to help you the next time someone makes your blood boil.

1. Any time you are having a conversation standing up, practice the "Natural Stance."

2. At the end of every encounter, shake the other person's hand.[1]

3. Practice your REAL Listening (see Lesson 16).

---

[1]   Unless, of course, you're in the middle of a viral pandemic, in which case a confident wave from six feet away will have to do!

Leadership Education & Application Passport

Part A – *Work with your leadership mentor to complete the Target Outcome and Actions sections below.*

Skill: Maintaining Professionalism Under Pressure

Target Outcome: With whom will you be applying this skill and what are you hoping to accomplish?

_____

_____

_____

_____

Actions: What actions need to be taken before and during the application of this skill?

- _____
- _____
- _____
- _____
- _____

Part B – *Now, take a moment with your leadership mentor to review the results and explore what you took away from this experience of "Stop, Drop, and Roll." Look for ways to improve your ongoing experiences when keeping your cool during conflict.*

Results:

- _____

- _____

- _____

- _____

- _____

Takeaways:

- _____

- _____

- _____

- _____

- _____

Once you have completed Parts A and B above, have your leadership mentor initial and date the stamp for this Lesson.

Congratulations! You are one step closer to being the leader you've always dreamed of being.

LEADERSHIP EDUCATION & APPLICATION PASSPORT

CONTINUE 2 IMPROVE

Initials: _____
Date: _____

"It's hard for me to come up with a plan and hold my players accountable until I self-evaluate and hold myself accountable."

— *Dabo Swinney*

LESSON 19

Get 'er Done

Creating a Culture of Accountability

In today's chaotic business environment, being able to hold others accountable is a key leadership differentiator that will fuel your success and that of the organization. When you don't hold team members accountable for poor behavior, missed deadlines or weak performance, your own credibility will be tarnished. Why is accountability important? In a 2019 article published in *Medium*, Darius Foroux, founder of The Sounding Board, shared the results of his procrastination survey. He found that 88% of the 2,219 participants admitted to procrastinating for at least one hour a day.[1] If those five hours a week could have been applied to one workplace task but you chose to fritter them away, how might that choice have negatively impacted that one project?

I've taken several online certification programs; some span 6 weeks, some take 8 weeks, and some even 12 weeks of engagement to

---

1   https://medium.com/darius-foroux/how-common-
    is-procrastination-a-study-80869467c3f3

complete. The very best of those programs had two things in common: assignments and accountability. When I took the 12-week World Class Speaking Coach Certification Program, we met every Thursday evening. At the end of every session, we had an assignment that needed to be completed by the next meeting. My accountability buddy and I decided to meet every Monday afternoon. What I found was that we both had our assignments completed in time to share at our accountability meeting; we never wanted to let each other down. Assignments and accountability go hand-in-hand. When you know you are scheduled to meet with someone on a regular basis to share your progress, odds are that you'll have that assignment completed before the due date.

Ideally, leaders get people to do what they want, when they want, because the worker wants to. When people do what you want because they want to, they are self-accountable. When they don't get it done, you have to be prepared to hold them accountable for getting it done. Accountability is about setting expectations and developing a framework for ensuring people follow through on their commitments.

The Triple A Formula

To increase the level of responsibility when problems do occur, follow what I call the Triple A Formula for accountability:

- **Assessment** — Schedule reviews at regular intervals to ensure that each action item is being completed on time. If you wait until the project deadline, it will be too late to make adjustments that will keep the project on track. The interval for reviews depends on the deadline and the competence of the person completing the request. A tight deadline and a highly competent person will require less attention than a less competent person with a tight deadline.

- **Assignment** — During the reviews, you may identify additional steps that need to be completed or find that steps that were to be completed were not handled fully or at all. It then becomes necessary to reset expectations by making new assignments or reassigning certain steps. If someone lets you down, it's important to:
    - Restate exactly what it is you want
    - Establish a new deadline for the missed action items
    - Find out what resources they need to deliver on time.

Most leaders don't like conflict. But don't be like most leaders — have the courage to have those accountability conversations. When you set the expectation for a higher level of accountability, you'll have fewer disappointments.

Don't let your team members accept anything but their best and you'll get it. No matter how uncomfortable it may be for you (and them) in the beginning, in the end it will be better for everyone.

- **Answerability** — It's not enough for the responsible person to say, "I ran out of time" or "something suddenly came up."[2] Excuses are a way for people to deflect blame on to other people or other things so they don't have to take responsibility. They need to set aside the excuses and tell you how they plan to get back on track so the project does not fall behind. By getting them to own their responsibility and provide you with a plan, you are

---

2   "Something suddenly came up" is an excuse made famous by Marcia Brady in the fourth season of The Brady Bunch, in an episode entitled "The Subject Was Noses." To this day, this generic excuse continues to crop up in business for everything from cancelling a meeting at the last minute to not finishing a project by its deadline.

not only teaching them to be responsible, you are teaching them to think like a problem solver.

Without accountability, even the smartest, strongest, and hardest-working leaders will fail. They will fail to meet their organizational goals and objectives. They will fail to develop and coach their team members. They will fail the organization overall. Effective leaders understand the need to hold people accountable. Hold yourself accountable too!

Without accountability, even the smartest, strongest and hardest-working leaders will fail.

President Harry S. Truman had a sign on his desk that read: "The Buck Stops Here." The phrase refers to the fact that the President has to make the decisions and accept the ultimate responsibility for those decisions. As a leader, you too will find that the buck stops with you. Because here's the kicker: If you don't hold others accountable, you will become accountable for whatever slips through the cracks. Accountability goes beyond your team's actions. Leaders are accountable for the performance of their teams. Just like a nation's leader needs to take responsibility for his or her decisions, you have to be accountable for the actions (or lack of action) by your team members.

A critical part of any accountability process is the accountability meeting. At Toyota, I had a weekly staff meeting where everyone reviewed the status of their most pressing projects. To be effective, these meetings need to be structured and planned. The following is an outline you can use to guide these conversations.

"All work and no play make Jack a very dull boy," or so the saying goes. So, while a business agenda is important, people are vital.

Remember that anytime you are meeting with your team or with an employee or colleague one-on-one, you need to spend a few minutes building relationships before getting into the agenda. Then (and only then), tackle the agenda. Here's one that works well for me during accountability meetings:

- **Review the project objectives**

- **Assess progress**
  - What was to be done?
  - What was done?
  - Where is the person stuck?

- **Assign**
  - Set new dates for missed targets
  - Set targets for new tasks
  - What help or resources does the team member need?

- **Answerability**
  - If applicable, what will the team member do to prevent missing dates a second time?
  - Recap the session
  - Confirm commitments
  - Be accountable to your team member just as they are accountable to you — find out what they need from you
  - Confirm next meeting date and time.

Leaders who take the time to facilitate accountability meetings get more benefits and are more likely to achieve their goals and objectives faster and with less frustration. They have less stress, more engaged team members, and better project outcomes.

Leaders who take the time to facilitate accountability meetings get more benefits and are more likely to achieve their goals and objectives faster and with less frustration. They have less stress, more engaged team members and better project outcomes.

Reflection Question for Lesson 19: How did you model accountability today for your team members?

Time for a break! When you're ready, move ahead to another chapter/lesson and then come back to the following START Activity and Passport exercise during your second read-through of the book.

START Activity

————

Create a culture of accountability.

1. Create a pattern of regularly scheduled accountability meetings with your team members — as a team or one-on-one, depending on your needs and the needs of your team members.

2. If this is not something you do already, take time to let each of your team members know what your plan is and what information you expect during the meetings. Let them know in person and then follow up with an email.

3. Keep the meeting moving by writing down side issues in a parking lot and the names of your team members who need to deal with these issues.

4. Send the parking lot notes out so your team can add it to their action items.

Leadership Education & Application Passport

Part A – *Work with your leadership mentor to complete the Target Outcome and Actions sections below.*

Skill: Creating a Culture of Accountability

Target Outcome: With whom will you be applying this skill and what are you hoping to accomplish?

_____

_____

_____

_____

Actions: What actions need to be taken before and during the application of this skill?

- _____

- _____

- _____

- _____

- _____

Part B – *Now, take a moment with your leadership mentor to review the results and explore what you took away from this experience of holding others (and yourself) accountable. Look for ways to improve your ongoing experiences in this regard.*

Results:

- _____

- _____

- _____

- _____

- _____

Takeaways:

- _____

- _____

- _____

- _____

- _____

Once you have completed Parts A and B above, have your leadership mentor initial and date the stamp for this Lesson.

Congratulations! You are one step closer to being the leader you've always dreamed of being.

"We only get what we believe that we deserve. Raise the bar, raise your standards and you will receive a better outcome."

— *Joel Brown*

Does Your Coffee Taste Like Tea?

Establishing Strong Standards

If you are like me, one of the best parts of waking up is coffee in your cup. I like the bittersweet taste of coffee. I love the smooth, rich aroma of roasted coffee that fills the house. And I love the feel of a warm cup in my hand. That is, if the coffee is made right. Depending on how it's made, it can be weak, it can be strong, or it can be somewhere in between. While the strength of your coffee is purely a matter of preference, the strength of your standards is a matter of success. The stronger the standard, the easier it is for you and your team members to see problems. A lack of clear standards not only undermines performance and sabotages results within a team, it also negatively impacts engagement, relationships, and teamwork. There will be many occasions when you will need to set, agree to, and be guided by standards.

A lack of clear standards not only undermines performance and sabotages results within a team, it also negatively impacts engagement, relationships and teamwork.

Let's revisit the coffee example. My wife doesn't like coffee, so she never makes it. But one day, I was out of town and her sister came to visit. Her sister likes coffee. Uh oh! My wife sent me a text asking me how to make coffee. I sent back "8 cups of water and two scoops of coffee." When I got home that night, my sister-in-law gave me a hard time about my coffee recipe. She said my coffee tasted more like tea. The next morning, I asked my wife to show me how she made the coffee. After watching my wife measure the water and coffee, I immediately knew I had done a poor job of communicating how to make good coffee. Not only was the coffee weak, so were the standards I'd established.

Strong standards convey information to others in a simple and clear-cut manner. It's not only important for you to understand the standard or expectation, it's important for your team and everyone else involved. When the standard is strong and understood by everyone, the abnormal condition becomes easy to identify before it becomes a major issue. The definition of a problem is the difference between a standard and the current situation. Strong standards make it easy to see the problem but when the standard is weak, the problem is harder to see. For a standard to be strong, it must be:

- Specific

- Tangible and recognizable

- Quantifiable

- Shared and agreed to.

Strong standards make it easy to see the problem but when the standard is weak, the problem is harder to see.

Let's apply these criteria to our family coffee dilemma. On the surface, two scoops of coffee for 8 cups of water seems to meet all the requirements. However, two areas aren't specific enough to be recognizable. For instance, what do we mean by "cup?" Is this a standard measuring cup, a coffee cup (which come in various sizes), or is it a demarcation on the side of the coffee pot? In this case, we were both referring to the measurement on the side of the coffee pot. That leaves the scoop. What is a scoop? We both used the scoop that was in the coffee container but how did we use it? Did we make:

1. Level scoops

2. Rounded scoops

3. Heaping scoops

4. Or, in my case, *seriously heaping* scoops?

Of the four, which does a better job of meeting all the criteria for a strong standard? That's right: the level scoop. The level scoop is more tangible and makes it easier for others to recognize and repeat. I assumed she would measure the coffee the same way I did (overflowing, mountainous aromatic scoops) and we all know what happens when you assume.

Once you've refined your standard so that it is specific, tangible, and recognizable, share it. Ask yourself, "Who will be impacted by this standard?" Get feedback from those people to make *sure* it is specific, tangible and recognizable. You also share it for a second purpose — to ensure you gain their commitment and support. Keep in mind that this is not about getting their approval; it's about making the standard or expectation understandable by all those involved. You ultimately have the responsibility to decide on the final standard or expectation to be applied. Now that you've shared the standard, document it to ensure that you and your team are on the same page and committed to the new standard.

In a 2015 Gallup article, Jim Harter explains that about half of all workers don't know what is expected of them at work.[1] Clear standards and expectations (or a lack thereof) can make or break your team members' willingness to engage. Even if they are motivated, the lack of clear standards and expectations can have them working on the wrong priorities.

Like rules, standards are meant to be broken. Not really, but they don't live forever. At Toyota, our mentality was always "old way, new way, better way." Your standards need to evolve as time goes on, to ensure you are continuing to improve. Whether you're making coffee, defining a quality standard, providing instructions, or making a request, the more specific your words, the easier it will be for others to provide you with the outcome you desire.

Reflection Question for Lesson 20: What problems or issues did you encounter today? Did they jump out at you because standards made it easy to see the deviation, or did it burst in your face, catching you by surprise?

_____

_____

_____

_____

Time for a break! When you're ready, move ahead to another chapter/lesson and then come back to the following START Activity and Passport exercise during your second read-through of the book.

---

1   https://www.gallup.com/workplace/236567/obsolete-annual-reviews-gallup-advice.aspx

START Activity

Create strong standards that your team can understand.

1. Identify a situation at your workplace with no known standard.

2. Describe what you think is the best standard to put in place that will meet your internal/external customers' needs. Ensure it meets the criteria for a clear standard.

3. Document the standard and train everyone on the standard.

4. Apply the standard, check the results, and standardize it if it provides the necessary results.

Leadership Education & Application Passport

Part A – *Work with your leadership mentor to complete the Target Outcome and Actions sections below.*

Skill: Creating Strong Standards

Target Outcome: With whom will you be applying this skill and what are you hoping to accomplish?

_____

_____

_____

_____

Actions: What actions need to be taken before and during the application of this skill?

- _____

- _____

- _____

- _____

- _____

Part B – *Now, take a moment with your leadership mentor to review the results and explore what you took away from this experience of creating strong standards. Look for ways to improve your ongoing experiences in this regard.*

Results:

- _____
- _____
- _____
- _____
- _____

Takeaways:

- _____
- _____
- _____
- _____
- _____

Once you have completed Parts A and B above, have your leadership mentor initial and date the stamp for this Lesson.

Congratulations! You are one step closer to being the leader you've always dreamed of being.

"Sometimes even hearing a bad idea is a great way to get to a good idea."

— *Charlie Day*

That's Stupid

Responding to Bad Ideas

Have you ever been in a meeting where someone came up with an idea that seemed so ridiculous you couldn't help but laugh? I have, but I wasn't in a meeting. Instead, I was covered in sweat, using a push mower to cut our grass in 86-degree heat with 57% humidity. My daughter, Katie, said to me, "Dad — I don't think I should have to do chores. None of my friends have to."

Most ideas (at work and at home) fall between a stroke of genius and a complete flop. It may seem obvious to you when an idea should be sent directly to File 13 (i.e., the trash can), but it's not always so clear to the person submitting the idea. When you're leading a team, you can't come straight out and say how you feel about a bad idea. It's your job to develop people's abilities. How you respond to lousy ideas can have a significant impact on your team members' willingness to share future ideas.

Here is the rest of the story. After the initial shock wore off, I said, "Let me get this right, Katie. You want to live in this house, eat the food and wear the clothing your mother and I provide, sleep in a bed in a climate-controlled house, and do so without having to contribute in any way. Is that what I'm hearing?" With a slightly bowed head and a sad voice she said, "Yes."

I thought, "Okay," and then said, "If that is really what you want, that's fine but there will be a few changes. You'll need to take your pillow, a blanket, and your book bag and move into the workout room off the garage. We'll bring you three meals a day and you will be able to take a shower once a day. You will not have access to your phone or TV. You'll go to school and come straight home to work on your homework. How does that sound?" She paused. The rest of the conversation sounded a little something like this:

> **Katie:** "Not very good, Dad."
>
> **Me:** "Well, Katie, it's your choice. What do you want to do? Do you want to be part of the family or do you want to be left alone?"
>
> **Katie:** "I want to be part of the family."
>
> **Me:** "Good, now finish mowing the grass."

(Just kidding! I didn't make her mow the grass. I figured she felt bad enough — no sense rubbing salt in her wounds.)

Learning to Listen and Respond, Instead of Judging and Dismissing

Part of your job as a leader is to develop your team members and build their confidence. That means making an effort to include their thoughts and ideas when solving problems. It's great when they come up with creative and innovative ideas. Unfortunately, they are not always going to hit a homerun with every idea they share. So how do you respond to bad ideas when they rear their ugly heads?

Leaders, like parents, aren't perfect. You may be tempted to say, "That's stupid" or shame them like I did with Katie, but don't give in to temptation. I reacted the way I did because I was hot, sweaty, and frustrated after having worked a full day. That is no excuse — what I did was wrong. But it's easier to forgive in a personal situation than it is in an employment situation. A workplace is not, no matter how much it might seem like it, a family or a place where patriarchy or condescension have any place. At work, you are held to a higher standard. No matter how bad the idea is or how you may be feeling in the moment, you can never say or do anything to your people that will shut them down. How you respond to bad ideas can have a significant impact on your team members' morale and performance.

No matter how bad the idea is or how you may be feeling in the moment, you can never say or do anything to your people that will shut them down. How you respond to bad ideas can have a significant impact on your team members' morale and performance.

Fortunately, there is a six-step process I've found useful in turning bad ideas into good (or even great) ideas ... without shattering the team member's self-esteem:

1. Take time to understand the idea completely

2. Point out the positives

3. Express your concerns

4. Solicit/suggest ideas to overcome your concerns

5. Reposition the idea

6. Finalize and agree.

Bad Idea Example

Imagine you're in a work situation where a piece of equipment is being assembled, but the assembly worker can't reach the final bolt, which is above his head. Suddenly, he has an idea!

"With the changes to my process, I'm about four inches shy of being able to reach the last bolt. I think if I turn over a plastic parts tub and stand on it, I'll be okay."

1. **Take time to understand the idea completely:** Ask clarifying questions, like, "So, you think a parts tub will give you the height you need?"

2. **Point out the positives:** "I can see how the parts tub would allow you to reach the final bolt and be small enough that you could move it in and out of your way as needed."

3. **Express your concerns:** "I don't know that a plastic parts tub is the safest thing to stand on. I'm afraid you could get injured."

4. **Solicit/suggest ideas to overcome your concerns:** "What else could we do to allow you to reach the highest bolt?"

5. **Reposition the idea**: "I like your idea of a small wheeled step ladder that locks in place when you stand on it."

6. **Finalize and agree:** "I'll have Jerry work this process for the remainder of the day so those top bolts get addressed for now and I'll have Sue pick up the step ladder this afternoon so you will have it tomorrow."

By identifying the merits of the idea, you are maintaining their confidence. When you guide them to find alternatives, you are developing their future problem-solving skills.

If you want great ideas, you have to create an environment where all team members know their ideas will be considered. If you follow these steps, you'll ensure your team members will keep trying. Who knows? Someone on your team may come up with the next game-changing idea for your department or organization!

If you want great ideas, you have to create an environment where all team members know their ideas will be considered.

Reflection Question for Lesson 21: What was the last "bad idea" you heard and how did you react to it?

_____

_____

_____

_____

Time for a break! When you're ready, move ahead to another chapter/lesson and then come back to the following START Activity and Passport exercise during your second read-through of the book.

START Activity

―――――――

Responding to Bad Ideas

Throughout this book, I've stressed the need for one-on-one meetings under various conditions. During those sessions, there will be opportunities for your team members to share ideas and possible solutions. Most ideas are rarely perfect. Use the 6-step process for responding to bad ideas to turn average ideas into great ideas.

Leadership Education & Application Passport

Part A – *Work with your leadership mentor to complete the Target Outcome and Actions sections below.*

Skill: Responding to Bad Ideas

Target Outcome: With whom will you be applying this skill and what are you hoping to accomplish?

_____

_____

_____

_____

Actions: What actions need to be taken before and during the application of this skill?

- _____

- _____

- _____

- _____

- _____

Part B – *Now, take a moment with your leadership mentor to review the results and explore what you took away from the experience of trying the 6-step process for responding to bad ideas. Look for ways to improve your ongoing experiences in this regard.*

Results:

- _____

- _____

- _____

- _____

- _____

Takeaways:

- _____

- _____

- _____

- _____

- _____

Once you have completed Parts A and B above, have your leadership mentor initial and date the stamp for this Lesson.

Congratulations! You are one step closer to being the leader you've always dreamed of being.

"Words are singularly the most powerful force available to humanity. We can choose to use this force constructively with words of encouragement, or destructively using words of despair. Words have energy and power with the ability to help, to heal, to hinder, to hurt, to harm, to humiliate and to humble."

— *Yehuda Berg*

One Size Does Not Fit All

Delivering Effective Feedback

Barney Fife is famous for saying, "Nip it, nip it, nip it!" — invoking the concept of "nipping it in the bud" when you see something suboptimal that needs to be brought to a halt. Unfortunately, there are many leaders who are afraid to "nip it" when it comes to confronting performance issues. Why are leaders reluctant to give performance feedback? The number one reason for the reluctance stems from the worry that the team member will have a serious emotional reaction to the feedback. Another reason leaders are reluctant is their fear of conflict. Giving employee feedback is a delicate process. When done correctly, it brings problems to light so they can be solved.

Giving employee feedback is a delicate process. When done correctly, it brings problems to light so they can be solved.

When you don't "nip it" when you observe poor performance, you are giving implicit permission for the poor performance to continue. You are also missing out on an opportunity to build trust by confronting the issue and working with the team member to resolve the problem. Failing to give performance feedback leads to negative consequences — not only for the company but the person who needs it and for the leader who should deliver it. You need to learn how to deliver feedback in a way that will improve and grow your team members, and, ultimately, the business.

What is the right way to give employee feedback? You've probably heard the saying — "you can catch more flies with honey than with vinegar." That is not necessarily the case when it comes to feedback. It depends on the person's level of competence as it relates to the task being performed. People with a low level of competence in a task are more likely to prefer a sweeter, gentler approach whereas people with a high level of competence in a task generally appreciate the bitter truth or direct approach. Let's explore the two types of feedback and how they can impact a person depending on their level of competence in relation to a task.

Validation — Team members with a low level of task competence prefer their feedback to be success-based. This makes complete sense, if you think about it. We often lack confidence when exposed to new tasks. When leaders provide success-based feedback, we are building the team member's confidence

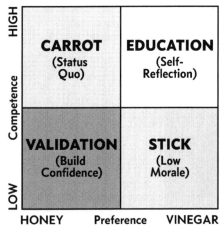

and helping to maintain a higher level of commitment toward the task. One way to provide validation while ensuring continual growth for team members with low competence levels is to use the "What I Liked/Next Time" method of feedback. Start the feedback by stating one element you liked, being specific about the situation and why you liked it. Follow that with a suggested action they might try next time to bring their performance to another level. I use this form of feedback when I coach emerging speakers on their presentations. For example: If a speaker is moving all over the stage area without purpose, I would say, "Jim, I really like how you are not afraid to use the entire stage. One thing I think you can do next time to take your presentation to the next level is to designate a place on the stage for each of your stories so you can move to each location with powerful purpose." When it comes to giving validating feedback, the idea is to elevate the performance, not to overwhelm the performer.

Stick — Was there ever a time when you were having difficulty learning a new skill and someone provided you feedback based on your failures? How did it make you feel? Imagine how the person in the previous example would feel if you took a more direct approach to that situation. "Jim, when I see you pacing back and forth on the stage, you remind of an anxious caged lion. You are not projecting confidence in yourself or your content." As you might expect, team members with a low level of task competence may feel as though you are hitting them over the head with a stick. This will naturally lower their morale and reduces their commitment to mastering the new task.

Carrot — You might think that giving success-based feedback — regardless of the competence level of the person receiving the feedback — would be the preferred focus. In fact, providing success-based feedback to a team member with a high level of competence can lead to a "status quo" level of performance — which, over time, can result in disengaged team members or attrition. When most people get good at something, they are not satisfied with the status quo. They want to be challenged so they can get to that next level. Giving them a reward or treat (the proverbial carrot) when they have done what they consider just a "good enough" job can demotivate them from doing even more.

Education — Highly competent people need education over validation to feel as though they are growing and thriving. If you focus on successes and have no real advice on how highly competent performers can improve, you are doing them a disservice. By providing failure-based feedback, you are introducing a challenge they feel they must overcome. The process of delivering feedback to this group is similar to the "What I Liked/Next Time" method — the key being that instead of identifying a success that can be improved, you identify a point of failure. Instead of making a suggestion for the next time, ask the team member for their ideas about what they could do to take their performance to a new level. If they are at a loss, *then* make a suggestion.

6 Levels of Expertise and the 3-Part Factual Statement

To determine a person's task competence, think about how much effort you would have to put into coaching that person on a failure for a specific task. On the Coaching Interaction Scale, a Level 1 is an expert and a Level 6 is a beginner:

- Level #1 – Inform team member that a problem exists

- Level #2 – Identify a specific discrepancy

- Level #3 – Help team member reach a resolution

- Level #4 – Suggest corrective actions if the team member can't come up with any on their own

- Level #5 – Demonstrate the corrective action

- Level #6 – Provide formal training on the corrective action

Regardless of the feedback focus, feedback should always be offered in a constructive, encouraging, collaborative, and supporting environment. That begs the question, "How do you identify a point of failure in a positive way?" I suggest you do it by using what's called the "Three-Part Factual Statement" — the formula explained in Lesson 4 of this book. Begin by clearly identifying the issue or point of failure. This is the tricky part because you want to focus on the *problem* — not the person. The second element requires that you describe your emotional reaction to the person's failure. The last element is about sharing the source of your emotional reaction.

Feedback should always be offered in a constructive, encouraging, collaborative and supporting environment.

For example: "When the payroll is not entered by 11:00 a.m. on Mondays, I get antsy because It doesn't give me much time to run all of the payroll reports before the noon transmittal deadline." In this example, it is clear that my focus was on the problem not the person. It also makes my emotional state clear to the team member and the reason for that emotional reaction.

Stop applying a one-size-fits-all approach when it comes to employee feedback. Before giving feedback, take the time to evaluate the competence level of your team members when it comes to each task. Adjusting your style to meet their specific needs will result in team members who are happier, more productive, and more engaged.

Reflection Question for Lesson 22: Think of the most difficult task in your department. Where on the Coaching Interaction Scale does each of your team members fall?

_____

_____

_____

_____

Time for a break! When you're ready, move ahead to another chapter/lesson and then come back to the following START Activity and Passport exercise during your second read-through of the book.

START Activity

Effective Feedback

1. For each of your team members, identify a specific situation where you can apply the What I Liked/Next Time method of feedback, and plan to deliver it this week.

2. Write the What I Liked/Next Time statements.

3. Deliver the feedback to each team member in a constructive, encouraging, collaborative, and supporting environment.

Leadership Education & Application Passport

Part A – *Work with your leadership mentor to complete the* *Target Outcome and Actions sections below.*

Skill: Delivering Effective Feedback

Target Outcome: With whom will you be applying this skill and what are you hoping to accomplish?

_____

_____

_____

_____

Actions: What actions need to be taken before and during the application of this skill?

- _____

- _____

- _____

- _____

- _____

Part B – Now, take a moment with your leadership mentor to review the results and explore what you took away from this experience of delivering customized, effective feedback. Look for ways to improve your ongoing experiences in this regard.

Results:

- _____

- _____

- _____

- _____

- _____

Takeaways:

- _____

- _____

- _____

- _____

- _____

Once you have completed Parts A and B above, have your leadership mentor initial and date the stamp for this Lesson.

Congratulations! You are one step closer to being the leader you've always dreamed of being.

"You can be like a thermometer, just reflecting the world around you. Or you can be a thermostat, one of those people who sets the temperature."

— *Cory Booker*

The Daily News

Taking the Company's Emotional Temperature

At Toyota, even before I was in leadership, I was required to go out on the shop floor every day and interact with the team members. As a leader, I continued this practice because I found it so meaningful. When was the last time you went out on the shop floor or waded through the cubicle farm and talked one-on-one with team members to take the emotional temperature of the organization? And I'm not talking about just your direct reports. If you're like most busy managers and VPs, it's been a while since you've visited the place where the work is actually done. For some of you, perhaps you've never done this at all. Meeting individually with team members in their work environment is an incredibly powerful, motivating, and impactful way to build trusting relationships and understand the emotions flowing through your organization.

Meeting individually with team members in their work environment is an incredibly powerful, motivating and impactful way to build trusting relationships and understand the emotions flowing through your organization.

When I showed genuine interest in the team members and the work they were doing, they opened up and sometimes they would actually let me try parts of their jobs. One time when I worked at the Toyota Forklift plant, a team member in Mast Welding let me tack weld a few spots on a forklift mast. It was a great way for me to be "one of the guys" on the team during that moment.

I've seen many managers develop meaningful connections with their teams by interacting daily in this way. I recall that one manager, who was assigned to the machining department, knew one team member's wife loved Betty Boop. One weekend, the manager went to Nashville, Indiana — best known as an arts-and-crafts tourist destination (a.k.a. all things knick-knacky) — and came across a shop full of Betty Boop figurines. Imagine the look on the team member's face on Monday when the manager said, "John, I came across this amazing collection of Betty Boop figurines in Nashville. I remember you telling me how much your wife loves Betty Boop so I bought this one and thought she might like it." How did that gesture impact their future relationship? How did it impact the emotional temperature of the organization? This team member felt seen and acknowledged on a truly personal level.

DAILY One-on-One Check-ins

What is the purpose of conducting daily one-on-one check-ins? The first — and probably most important — purpose for checking in every day is to learn about your workforce. Taking the time to learn about team members shows you believe they are valuable and worth knowing. When a leader takes the time to invest in team members on a more personal level, especially those he or she wouldn't normally interact with during meetings, it shows that he or she cares about who their team members are — not just that they show up and do their work.

I'd like you to think of "daily" check-ins using a helpful acronym: DAILY. Another purpose of DAILY one-on-one check-ins is to take the emotional temperature of the organization. As a leader, you may think everything is going well in your organization — that your team members are happy and motivated. But are they? Too many companies find out too late that their team members are upset or disgruntled. One way to avoid this is through DAILY one-on-one check-ins. Go see how they feel about their jobs, the company, their leaders. Knowing how *everyone* feels about these areas can tell you whether any issues you identify are company-wide feelings or just isolated to pockets within the organization.

Let's go deeper. What is a DAILY One-on-One Check-in? DAILY is an acronym that stands for:

- **Devote** time

- Show **Appreciation**

- Show **Interest**

- **Listen**

- Be **You**-Focused.

Devote time – Set aside part of your day for relationship building. At Toyota, we were expected to spend a minimum of 30 minutes each day performing one-on-one check-ins. These short, face-to-face interactions help build a foundation of good working relationships.

Appreciation – Don't just wait for someone to go above and beyond the call of duty; show appreciation for a job well done every day. Genuinely compliment team members when they do something well. Be positive; it will strengthen your relationships. During a daily one-on-one check-in is not the time to talk with team members about being tardy that morning.

Interest – Find out what is going well and what is not going well —
both professionally and personally. Keep in mind that it may take
people a while to open up to you personally. Just let that happen
naturally. But don't be afraid to ask questions about work-related
issues. The more you show interest in an employee's work life, the
easier it will be for them to open up about their personal life. It
will most likely start by them telling you their child won the t-ball
championship or some other personal event they are excited about
or proud of. As time goes on, they may trust you with other, more
emotional issues. We've all heard the saying, "Leave home at home
and work at work." You can say it until you are blue in the face
but it's impossible, and it's not an "ideal" we should strive for. We
are each but one person with one brain and one heart. No matter
how hard people try to keep the two separate, it is only a matter of
time before one impacts the other. That's not a bad thing. Which
brings me to "L."

Listen – Practice REAL Listening (see Lesson 16) during your
one-on-one check-ins. The idea is not to get caught up in their
personal life issues but to show you care. When they are sharing
extremely personal issues, you may just want to nod your head know-
ingly. They are most likely not looking for you to give them an answer,
just understanding and implied emotional support. When it comes to
sensitive personal issues, the best advice you can give them is to seek
assistance from the company Employee Assistance Program (EAP).
By listening more than talking, you'll quickly become known as
someone who can be trusted. Be the leader they deserve, listen with
respect, and do your best to support them.

Be **You**-Focused – As a speaker, one of the lessons I have learned
is the importance of what's called the I/You Ratio. Make your
one-on-one interactions more about the team member and less
about you. During your one-on-one check-ins, pay attention to your

I/You Ratio. Listen to how many times you say "I" or "me" versus "you" or "your." A good I/You Ratio is 1:3.

Who Should Perform DAILY One-on-One Check-ins?

At Toyota, we had three groups that conducted daily one-on-one check-ins. The first level included all the assistant team leaders and team leaders. The second level included anyone in an internal customer support department. The third level included assistant managers and above. As a leader, you should find it fairly easy to make time to check in with all your direct team members. Obviously, face-to-face is ideal. However, if you are traveling (or if your work operation is spread out across multiple geographies, or if you're in the midst of a pandemic), you can do it virtually.

At Toyota, "internal customer support" refers to anyone who works in a support department like finance, HR, employee relations, safety, purchasing, organizational development, engineering, etc. An internal customer is a team member who actually produces the product or service for your *external* customers. In many cases, they do not have the freedom to leave their work area except during scheduled breaks and lunches. They should not be expected to use breaks and lunch to handle issues like payroll issues, benefits, or any other similar issues. As such, they need to be cared for just as you would care for your external customers. This would require people working in finance, HR, safety, etc. to get out from behind their desks to check in on those team members who are tied to a process that can't be left unattended.

The third level represents your assistant managers and above. At the Toyota Forklift plant, each person at these levels was assigned a specific department outside of their area of responsibility. At the end of the day, this level would collect all the data from the other two levels and share their findings at the Drive Team Meeting. The Drive Team Meeting was a stand-up meeting where management took turns sharing their findings with the group and developing strategies to address any issues. The purpose was to gauge the overall emotional temperature of the organization to ensure that leaders were being attentive to their internal customers as much as they were focused on external customers. When you make time for DAILY one-on-one check-ins with your team members, you will build trust and have them rallying around you when times are difficult.

Reflection Question for Lesson 23: How much time do you take every day interacting with the *internal* customers — the people who build the product or deliver the service that the external customer is willing to pay for?

_____

_____

_____

_____

Time for a break! When you're ready, move ahead to another chapter/lesson and then come back to the following START Activity and Passport exercise during your second read-through of the book.

START Activity

Taking the Company's Emotional Temperature

1. Spend at least 20 minutes a day for a month with the internal customer.

2. Document your findings daily.

3. At the end of the month, answer honestly: "How would you evaluate the emotional temperature of the company?"

4. Encourage any internal customers who may need professional assistance to seek HR assistance.

5. Address any safety concerns immediately.

Leadership Education & Application Passport

Part A – *Work with your leadership mentor to complete the Target Outcome and Actions sections below.*

Skill: Taking the company's emotional temperature through regular check-ins.

Target Outcome: With whom will you be applying this skill and what are you hoping to accomplish?

_____

_____

_____

_____

Actions: What actions need to be taken before and during the application of this skill?

- _____
- _____
- _____
- _____
- _____

Part B – *Now, take a moment with your leadership mentor to review the results and explore what you took away from this experience of DAILY One-on-One Check-ins. Look for ways to improve your ongoing experiences in this regard.*

Results:

- _____

- _____

- _____

- _____

- _____

Takeaways:

- _____

- _____

- _____

- _____

Once you have completed Parts A and B above, have your leadership mentor initial and date the stamp for this Lesson.

Congratulations! You are one step closer to being the leader you've always dreamed of being.

"A punishment to some, to some a gift, and to many a favor."

— *Lucius Annaeus Seneca*

No Good Deed Goes Unpunished

Learning to Use — Not Abuse — Strengths

The most recent dogs my wife and I have loved and lost were named Tess and Quilla (Kee-La). Together, they were sassy and hilarious, always doing funny and sometimes diabolical things to each other. For instance, if Tess wanted on the couch — where Quilla was lying down — Tess would go to the window and make a low huffing sound. That's all it would take to get Quilla to jump off the couch and protect our home from imaginary intruders. Having created a diversion to get Quilla off the couch, Tess would steal the comfy spot from her sister. You see, Quilla was a good guard dog — it was one of her many strengths — and Tess was great at using Quilla's strengths against her so she could get what she wanted (Quilla's spot on the couch). Smart girl!

This tendency to have your strengths used against you is perhaps even more prevalent among humans than it is with dogs. We see it at work all the time. As a leader, you probably have a mix of the five employee types that are explained in Lesson 26 about the "Attitude of Gratitude." If you're like most leaders, you have that "go to" person you always rely on to get those tough projects and tasks accomplished. Taking advantage of your "go to" person's strengths can be a sign of poor leadership. Isn't it time you flipped the switch and stop punishing your star performers?

If you're like most leaders, you have that "go to" person you always rely on to get those tough projects and tasks accomplished. Taking advantage of your "go to" person's strengths can be a sign of poor leadership. Isn't it time you flipped the switch and stop punishing your star performers?

There are far too many leaders out there who will take advantage of their top performers' strengths so they can get what they want. Some do it intentionally and others do it out of unconscious habit. Most workers are eager to do a good job. In the TWI Job Relations Training program, one of the four foundations for remarkable working relationships is "to make the best use of your employee's strengths." Making the best use of a person's strengths does not mean you should take undue advantage of someone's strengths, talents, or skills to get what you want. When leaders know an employee's strengths and continually go to that person to handle the most difficult and time-sensitive projects, it becomes a form of punishment.

The first type of "performance punishment" happens when the leader piles task after task on the self-starter, knowing she has superior skills and abilities as well as a great work ethic. Her high level of skill and work ethic is rewarded by giving her more work. The leader may say something like, "You have a bright future with the company. You just need to be patient a little longer." Eventually, the self-starter realizes that her leader has no intention of helping her advance. She realizes the leader is weak and needs the self-starter's skills and work ethic in order to continue to look good to their own boss.

The second type of "performance punishment" happens when the superstar is not only doing her own work but the work of others on the team. A weak leader will punish the superstar by pushing work from a poor performer to the superstar when the poor performer can't get it done on time. It sounds something like this, "I know you're busy, but can you get with Joe and help him get his project back on track? We are behind the eight ball, and I know I can depend on you to get the project back on schedule." The leader is right — everything will get done on time, but at what cost? What does the superstar have to do to get it all done? Maybe, she skips her lunch and breaks. Maybe, she works late every night to make sure it all gets done. Maybe, she skips going to a play with her mom.

However, that's just one side of the coin. What about the poor performers who get to eat lunch, go home on time, and go to their child's ball game? What did they learn? They learned that poor performance is acceptable and sometimes even rewarding. By doing as little as possible, they train the leader to:

- Give them less work

- Set lower targets and performance standards for them

- Promote them so they can become someone else's problem

- Give them overtime to allow them to complete tasks.

The question is, "What do you do as a leader to stop punishing good performers and stop rewarding poor performers?" You should be looking for strengths not being used by poor performers and leveling up poor performers to the same level of competence as your top performers. This not only helps the organization, but it also helps improve team member engagement and overall job satisfaction. If you don't want to burn out your top performers or drive them away, you have to recognize when you are punishing performance.

 ## Performance Punishing

Let's take a quick assessment! Look at the list below and write "YES" or "NO" in each blank.

You might be unintentionally punishing employees if ...

1. _____ You reward performance with an even more challenging project.

2. _____ You say things like, "You are the only one I can count on to get this done."

3. _____ You take work from poor performers and give it to your "go to" person.

4. _____ You have team members who rarely take breaks/lunch.

5. _____ You have team members who have a large number of vacation days banked.

6. _____ You give your top-performing team member the jobs no one else wants to do.

7. _____ You expect some team members to work harder and faster.

8. _____ You pay top performers the same as poor performers for the same job.

9. _____ You give less training to top performers because they are too valuable to release for professional development activities.

10. _____ You give your top perfomers less of your time and, therefore, less coaching and mentoring.

How did you do? Did you answer *yes* more than you answered *no*? If so, what are you going to do about it? If you do nothing, your superstars will get tired of always having to work harder, always having to pick up some else's slack, and never seeing any reward. Even if you reward and appreciate their extra efforts, they will eventually become discouraged when they realize their poor-performing coworkers can do as they please.

Here are four questions *great* leaders ask their team members:

"How are you doing?" – The purpose you aim to serve in asking this first question is to initiate a productive conversation. You want to discover how satisfied and how confident your people are in their work. Being asked to share may seem foreign to your team members at first, especially because most leaders don't ask. Your people may be thinking, "Is he serious?" or "If I answer honestly, can I trust him or will he hold it against me later?" Your team members need to know you are serious about hearing their views. They not only need to know you have the best interest of the organization at heart — they need to know you care about *them* as well. You've heard the phrase "I've got your back." Well, your team members need to know you have theirs.

"What is making your job harder to do?" — The typical response to this question is "nothing." Don't be one of those leaders who takes that at face value and walk away. You need to encourage your team members to open up, especially when it comes to the obstacles that are getting in their way. Asking these questions is not an exercise in checking off some boxes. So, don't fall for the "no news is good news" response. Dig deeper by asking questions about specific areas of their jobs.

"What would you like to see done?" — Once you get them to open up about how they are doing and the obstacles getting in their way, it's time to put your reputation on the line. Asking them for their ideas is not just about making them feel involved; it's about respecting their thoughts, feelings, and opinions. They may not come up with the perfect solutions and that's okay. Your job is to help them see their fledgling, imperfect idea in a new light by coaching them to see what could improve it (and even what is "wrong" with it) and how to overcome your concerns. You pick up a specific strategy in this regard in Lesson 21, about "Responding to Bad Ideas." (If you aren't reading this book chronologically and haven't seen it yet, you might want to skip to that lesson tomorrow!)

"Is there anything I can do right now to help?" — This last question is designed to provide your team members with immediate relief from some obstacle that may be impeding their progress at that time, if possible. If you want engaged, committed team members, you need to ask the question and then take action to show your level of commitment. Talk is cheap — merely asking these questions is not enough. Your team members will expect you to take action. And you owe it to them to at least try.

Reflection Question for Lesson 24: Based on your level of control, where can you do better to ensure job tasks and responsibilities are more equitably distributed?

_____

_____

_____

_____

Time for a break! When you're ready, move ahead to another chapter/lesson and then come back to the following START Activity and Passport exercise during your second read-through of the book.

START Activity

Learn to use, not abuse, the individual strengths of your team members.

Make copies of the following worksheet and have each team member answer the questions. Make sure they do not put their name on the form. The purpose is to see how they honestly feel. Summarize all responses into one document and identify the areas of greatest concern. Then meet one-on-one with each team member and ask the four questions described in this Lesson.

Worksheet

Is my leader unintentionally punishing employees? Mark "yes" or "no."

1. _____ My leader rewards my performance with an even more challenging project.

2. _____ My leader says things like, "You are the only one I can count on to get this done."

3. _____ My leader takes work from poor performers and gives it to me.

4. _____ I rarely get to take breaks/lunch because I'm too busy.

5. _____ I rarely take vacation because I have too much to do.

6. _____ My leader gives me the dirty jobs no one else wants to do.

7. _____ My leader expects more out of me than he/she does of the rest of the team.

8. _____ I work harder than others who get the same or greater pay.

9. _____ I never get to go to training or professional development activities because my boss can't get along without me.

10. _____ My leader never (or rarely) provides me with the coaching or mentoring I need.

Leadership Education & Application Passport

Part A – *Work with your leadership mentor to complete the Target Outcome and Actions sections below.*

Skill: Learning to Use, Not Abuse, Team Members' Strengths

Target Outcome: With whom will you be applying this skill and what are you hoping to accomplish?

_____

_____

_____

_____

Actions: What actions need to be taken before and during the application of this skill?

- _____

- _____

- _____

- _____

- _____

Part B – *Now, take a moment with your leadership mentor to review the results and explore what you took away from an honest exploration of whether you're punishing your superstars and rewarding your weak links. Look for ways to improve your ongoing experiences in this regard.*

Results:

- _____

- _____

- _____

- _____

- _____

Takeaways:

- _____

- _____

- _____

- _____

- _____

Once you have completed Parts A and B above, have your leadership mentor initial and date the stamp for this Lesson.

Congratulations! You are one step closer to being the leader you've always dreamed of being.

"No man will make a great leader who wants to do it all himself or get all the credit for doing it."

— *Andrew Carnegie*

The Goldfish Principle

Laying the Foundation for Success

Think back on a time when you implemented an idea, suggestion, or countermeasure only to find it floating, belly up, in the fishbowl of failed ideas. Ugh. Perhaps the death knell for your well-implemented idea was failure to first get necessary buy-in. Getting buy-in that lasts is critical to your project success. Too many times, we try to implement ideas in isolation even though — with few exceptions — the success of those ideas depends on the support of others.

After working in Training and Development at Toyota Motor Manufacturing Kentucky (TMMK), I moved to Toyota Industrial Equipment Manufacturing (TIEM) in Columbus, Indiana. A few weeks into my new position, I put together a comprehensive organizational development proposal with action steps and dates. I remember the excitement I felt as I hit "send" on the email that would distribute my proposal to all the managers and executives. The ideas I proposed were largely based on my experience at TMMK, and I just knew my new colleagues were going to love it.

After a few days of nothing but the sound of crickets since the distribution of my organizational development proposal, I went to each of the managers — one-by-one — to find out why they hadn't replied. Overall, they liked the idea behind the proposal but had their own ideas and suggestions for making it better. These were ideas I could have captured in my plan to make it *our* plan, if only I had followed an important concept: "The Goldfish Principle."

The Goldfish Principle is an informal process of quietly laying the foundation for some proposed idea, change, countermeasure, or project by thoughtfully and methodically gathering support and feedback from the stakeholders. It is an important element in any major change and should be pursued long before any formal steps are taken. Checking in with a key stakeholder prior to the proposal meeting — and gaining their buy-in — develops trust and helps you avoid being blindsided during the presentation.

Here's why they call it the Goldfish Principle ... If you've ever been to a pet store that sells fish, you've seen people holding plastic bags half full of water containing a goldfish or some other fish — like a beta or a clownfish. If that fish is not properly acclimated before placing it in its new home, it can get ill or even die. The same is true for your ideas. If your idea is not properly acclimated to the needs of the stakeholders and organization, it will die. There are two basic steps you need to take to acclimate a fish or idea to its new environment, warming the water and adjusting the pH.

Warming the Water — When you float the bag containing the goldfish in the fishbowl or tank, the temperature of the water in the bag is slowly brought to the same temperature as that of the new environment. In most business situations, you'll need to get stakeholders "warmed up" to your ideas before they are willing to support them. The best way for you to promote a proposal or course of action is to seek out those you believe will be key decision-makers and stakeholders. This should be done early in the creative process to ensure they have a sense of ownership when the final approval is requested.

If you want to work effectively with your senior leaders, you need to avoid surprises. The best way to do this is to hold "the meeting before the meeting." Ask each of your stakeholders for a short 15- to 20-minute one-on-one meeting so you can give them a glimpse of what your idea is before the final presentation and sign-off. This gives you a chance to hear their concerns and any suggestions they may have for your proposal. It allows you to make improvements and even major pivots before the big unveiling to the full group.

Adjusting the pH — Let's go back to our new fish, floating in his plastic bag inside the fish tank. After the bag is at the proper temperature, it's time to add half a cup of water from the fish tank to the bag. This process is repeated every 10 minutes until the bag is full. When you add water from the fish tank or bowl, you are slowly changing the pH of the water in the bag to match that of the new environment. This prevents the fish from going into shock and possibly dying. Imagine, if you will, the ability to adjust the pH (or attitude or overall vibe) of an organization, team, or group of people, as you can with water for your fish. You must slowly add input from the organization into your proverbial "plastic bag" of your ideas if you want buy-in that lasts. High-ranking people not only expect to be made aware of a new proposal prior to an official meeting, they expect to have input. If they find out about something for the first time during the meeting, they will feel they've been ignored or blindsided and could reject your ideas for that reason alone. So, it's important to approach these people one-on-one, sometimes multiple times, before the actual proposal is presented. This provides an opportunity to introduce the proposal to them and gauge their reaction to how you've included their ideas and suggestions for improving the proposal.

Once the water temperature has evened out and the pH has been adjusted, it's time for the goldfish to be released into the full tank or bowl so it can thrive in its new environment. Likewise, once you've mastered the art of "the meeting before the meeting," it's time for you to have your big meeting with all the stakeholders and get their full buy-in so your idea can flourish.

When I worked at Toyota, they called this process *Nemawashi*. In Japanese, it means the informal process for quietly laying the foundation for a proposed change or project by talking to all those concerned, gathering support and feedback. It is considered an important step in any major proposal. Successful *Nemawashi* enables changes to be carried out with the consent of all stakeholders.

The next time you have a big idea, schedule one-on-one meetings with each of the stakeholders and ask these five questions:

1. Does this proposal make sense to you?

2. Does this proposal fit in with our organizational goals?

3. What are your thoughts about it?

4. What ideas or suggestions do you have to make it more viable?

5. If I make the changes you suggest, will I be able to count on your support during the presentation?

Getting the answers to these questions will let you know if your proposal has a chance to thrive or if it will end up floating, belly up, in the fishbowl of failed ideas.

Reflection Question for Lesson 25: What was the last idea you had that needed approval from multiple stakeholders and how did you handle it?

_____

_____

_____

_____

Time for a break! When you're ready, move ahead to another chapter/lesson and then come back to the following START Activity and Passport exercise during your second read-through of the book.

START Activity

Apply the Goldfish Principle.

- Develop an implementation plan for a problem-solving effort, continuous improvement activity, company outing, or some other activity that requires multiple stakeholders' involvement.

- Schedule one-on-one meetings with each stakeholder.

- Share your proposal and ask the *five questions*:

    1. Does this proposal make sense to you?

    2. Does this proposal fit in with our organizational goals?

    3. What are your thoughts about it?

    4. What ideas or suggestions do you have to make it more viable?

    5. If I make the changes you suggest, will I be able to count on your support during the presentation?

Leadership Education & Application Passport

Part A – *Work with your leadership mentor to complete the Target Outcome and Actions sections below.*

Skill: Getting Buy-In Using the Goldfish Principle

Target Outcome: With whom will you be applying this skill and what are you hoping to accomplish?

_____

_____

_____

_____

Actions: What actions need to be taken before and during the application of this skill?

- _____

- _____

- _____

- _____

- _____

Part B – *Now, take a moment with your leadership mentor to review the results and explore what you took away from this experience of laying a foundation for success. Look for ways to improve your ongoing experiences in this regard.*

Results:

- _____
- _____
- _____
- _____
- _____

Takeaways:

- _____
- _____
- _____
- _____
- _____

Once you have completed Parts A and B above, have your leadership mentor initial and date the stamp for this Lesson.

Congratulations! You are one step closer to being the leader you've always dreamed of being.

"Appreciation can make a day — even change a life. Your willingness to put it into words is all that is necessary."

— *Margaret Cousins*

One Thing, Just One Thing

Developing an Attitude of Gratitude

I was recently going through some boxes when I came across my Air Force personnel file and a stack of papers that included letters of recognition and certificates that I received while I was serving. It made me realize how my leaders had a real attitude of gratitude — one I'm appreciative of still and one worthy of emulation.

Most leaders only recognize people when they have clearly gone above and beyond the call of duty, all the while those who are skating through the day or struggling to meet expectations are virtually invisible when it comes to recognition. My friend Cara Silletto, author of the book *Staying Power* and renowned expert on workplace retention, says, "Millennials don't want to be recognized for going above and beyond or the extra mile. What they really want to be recognized for is a job well done." In other words, as she puts it, "You need to thank me and pat me on the back for showing up five out of five days." In that same spirit, many of my letters of recognition in the Air Force were for doing my job. Granted, when your job is keeping nuclear weapons out of the hands of evildoers, you don't have room for mistakes. But it was still just for knowing and doing my job — for showing up to do what the Air Force was paying me to do.

Looking back, I can admit that I was not the perfect Airman when I first joined the Air Force. I was a high school dropout who had a chip on his shoulder. It wasn't until Master Sergeant Thomsen took the time to help me realize my potential that I found my true passion — I was born to be a trainer and he knew it. As a leader, it is your responsibility to help your workers realize their potential. Those letters of recognition and certificates raised me up and helped me become a better Airman. Eventually, Master Sergeant Thomsen sent me to school to become a trainer. As our Flight's trainer, it was now my job to raise each Airman on my Flight up to the next level. What an honor and a privilege.

To be an attentive leader, you need to focus on and absorb critical information. This requires a highly developed sense of listening and observation, as well as a desire to serve. Do you remember the movie *City* Slickers with Billy Crystal and Jack Palance? In the movie, the characters go in search of meaning in the midst of their respective mid-life crises, and come to believe that there's "one thing" — one secret to their lives — that will bring them meaning and solve all their problems. As it turned out, that secret is different for everyone. But what if, as leaders, we flipped that around so that the "one thing" wasn't about you but about your employees? What if you found ways to lift them up and celebrate their contributions, every day? How would your employee feel if, after a stressful meeting, they sat down at their desk to find their favorite coffee or snack waiting for them?

To be an attentive leader, you need to focus on and absorb critical information. This requires a highly developed sense of listening and observation, as well as a desire to serve.

By listening and observing, you can discover ways to be of service to your employees. There is a difference between putting a cup of coffee on a desk and putting a cup of iced coffee with cream, 20 pumps of raspberry, and 20 and a half pumps of white mocha (an order I actually once overheard!) on the desk. One is a gesture and the other is genuine. Leaders create strong relationships — not only through their ability to listen but also through their ability to observe and express gratitude.

When you receive meaningful recognition, a chemical reaction takes place in your brain. Dopamine is released, which leads to feelings of satisfaction, pride, and happiness. Even though the impact of recognition can be explained by science, delivering recognition is more of an art. Remember, a happy employee is an engaged employee. So in addition to having "the one thing" focus on shining a light on your employees in a general and daily way, here are four more ways you can serve up employee recognition to get the dopamine flowing and the engagement growing: pair your praise to the performance, hit a high note with a handwritten note, spotlight superstar performance, and recharge workers when you reward retention.

Pair Your Praise to the Performance – Achieving the perfect pairing is rare, but you can optimize the experience and avoid obvious clashes when the scale of praise equals the employee's level of effort. Thanking an employee with a $25 gift card for looking beyond their normal scope of work and finding a way to save your organization $30,000 will hit some sour notes. Likewise, handing out $100 for picking up a piece of trash while walking through the plant is overkill. The idea is to reinforce your employees' good behaviors without making them over-confident and diminishing their drive to do better.

Hit a High Note with a Handwritten Note – You've probably sent hundreds of thank-you emails. When was the last time you hand-wrote (and mailed or hand-delivered) a note, thanking someone for a job well done? It is an authentic gesture that will be remembered for a long time. Don't get me wrong — I like when my clients pay me, but when I get a handwritten card, it leaves an impression. And it goes on my office wall, where I can see it every day. When you need to thank someone for an outstanding job, a handwritten note, emphasizing your appreciation for their efforts, is the way to go.

Spotlight Superstar Performance – One of the best times to praise employees is when they perform noteworthy accomplishments. Not everyone is a superstar all the time but everyone performs like a superstar some of the time. Looking for great ways to shine the spotlight on them? Do it during meetings and through company-wide emails or newsletters. It's all about communication ... it sends the message that you notice and appreciate extra effort.

Recharge Workers When You Reward Retention – In a day and age when 30% of your employees only stay three years or less,[1] a work anniversary is a perfect time to let your employees know you appreciate them and their work. A simple card and a cake can go a long way to encourage higher employee retention. Having a monthly anniversary celebration and sending individual cards in the mail to employee homes, thanking the workers and their families, is a lot more cost effective than the 15% to 25% percent

---

1   Dave Romero, "What's the Real Value of a Great Employee Onboarding Program?" Training Industry, February 16, 2017, https://trainingindustry.com/articles/ onboarding/whats-the-real-value-of-a-great-employee-onboarding-program/

of their annual salary that it can cost to replace them if they leave because they feel unappreciated.

None of these approaches or tactics — individually or combined — is the answer. The answer is building remarkable working relationships with your employees. But serving up employee praise that leads to people feeling satisfied and happy can make a difference. Research by Emily Heaphy and Marcial Losada shows that the difference between the most successful teams and the least successful teams is the ratio of positive to negative feedback. The highest-performing teams receive almost a 6:1 positive to negative ratio of feedback.[2]

So, if you want stronger working relationships with your employees, serve up employee praise to get the dopamine flowing and the engagement growing.

Reflection Question for Lesson 26: What was the last form of recognition or praise you gave to your team members?

_____

_____

_____

_____

Time for a break! When you're ready, move ahead to another chapter/lesson and then come back to the following START Activity and Passport exercise during your second read-through of the book.

2   Marcial Losada and Emily Heaphy, "The Role of Positivity and Connectivity in the Performance of Business Teams: A Nonlinear Dynamics Model," American Behavioral Scientist, Vol. 47, Issue 6, Feb., 1, 2004, pp. 740-765.

START Activity

Develop an attitude of gratitude.

Depending upon your level of leadership, there are limitations to how you can recognize and reward your team members. Here are four options to consider. I would strongly suggest you make the first two a part of your daily and weekly rituals.

1. **Show appreciation** – You can do this through intangible ways (handshakes, high fives, or words of praise and thanks) as well as tangible gestures (letters, certificates, and gift cards).

2. **Increase frequency** – While I was in the Air Force, I averaged one tangible form of recognition every month. Not only did it make me feel appreciated, it gave my supervisor a tangible history of my performance when it came time to write my annual performance evaluation. It allowed him to write an accurate descriptive performance evaluation that was both fair and equitable.

3. **Creative scheduling** – When possible, look for ways to provide work schedules that don't conform to the traditional 9-to-5. One way to do this is to involve workers from every level to come up with options that allow flexibility without compromising customer needs.

4. **Provide advancement** – When I was at Toyota Industrial Equipment Manufacturing, we had a relatively flat structure and only about 500 employees. Over time, if there were no opportunities for promotion, the self-starters and superstars would leave. To prevent that from happening, we created levels within each of the titles.

Leadership Education & Application Passport

Part A – *Work with your leadership mentor to complete the Target Outcome and Actions sections below.*

Skill: Developing an Attitude of Gratitude

Target Outcome: With whom will you be applying this skill and what are you hoping to accomplish?

_____

_____

_____

_____

Actions: What actions need to be taken before and during the application of this skill?

- _____

- _____

- _____

- _____

- _____

Part B – *Now, take a moment with your leadership mentor to review the results and explore what you took away from this experience of expressing regular gratitude to your team members. Look for ways to improve your ongoing experiences in this regard.*

Results:

- _____
- _____
- _____
- _____
- _____

Takeaways:

- _____
- _____
- _____
- _____
- _____

Once you have completed Parts A and B above, have your leadership mentor initial and date the stamp for this Lesson.

Congratulations! You are one step closer to being the leader you've always dreamed of being.

"Parents are the center of a child's solar system, even as an adult. My dad had a stronger gravitational pull than most, so his absence was bound to leave a deep and lasting void."

— *Justin Trudeau*

G-Force

Getting People to Gravitate Toward You

Canadian Prime Minister Justin Trudeau was talking about his father in the quote on the preceding page, but the same can and should be true of leaders — they are sometimes the center of organizations with strong gravitational pull. Great leaders will not only get their team members to gravitate toward them, they will draw others to them. When those leaders are no longer in your life, they will leave you a deep and lasting gift. For me, that leader was MSGT Ronald L. Thomsen; he saw the trainer inside of a high school dropout.

I was walking around a B-52 bomber in the middle of a snowstorm when MSGT Thomsen drove up to me. He rolled his window down about two inches and said, "Matthews, you are going to be our Flight's trainer. Report to my office after you've been relieved from post." That moment certainly changed my life for the better, but it wasn't just what he did for me that day that stands out in my mind. There were two qualities he had that made people gravitate toward him. First, he was a highly competent Security Policeman who knew the job inside and out. Second, he had the ability to connect and engage with others in a way that was authentic, positive, and inspiring.

Confidence, Competence and Connectivity

In grade school, we all learned that gravity is impacted by both distance and mass. As it turns out, your ability to get people to gravitate toward you (personally and professionally) is also based on distance and mass. It's called your G-Force Leadership Quotient. Your gravitational force increases as distance decreases. A leader's distance from their team members and those they interact with determines their LCS (Leadership Connectivity Score). When your LCS grows, you become approachable, pulling your team members closer to you. The question is, "How connected are you to your team members?" Keep in mind we are talking about connectivity or friendliness — not friendship in the traditional sense.

Your connectivity is often based on how others perceive your confidence, the degree to which you are calm and composed during crisis, and your willingness to interact with them on a more personal level. Leaders with a high LCS don't seek validation — they know their worth. They don't get flustered when some unplanned situation turns their plan upside-down. They like getting to know their team members and anyone else they interact with in the course of their work.

Gravitational force also increases as mass increases. A leader's "mass" is determined by their LCR (Leadership Competency Rating). When your LCR mass increases, your team members' confidence in you grows, pulling them closer to you. If the people you work with (and for) are impressed by your expertise, they will gravitate toward you. You can also increase your LCR by being a master of your trade and a Jack of many other trades outside of your expertise. This will allow you to engage with a wider circle of people on a variety of subjects.

Connecting in Many Circles

Take a look at the diagram provided here, showing how you're at the middle of concentric circles of stakeholders of all kinds. As a leader, you not only represent your team, you represent the entire organization. You will be interacting with other coworkers (which include your bosses) and, depending upon your responsibilities, you could be interacting with visitors and outside agencies, as well as other people you come in contact with during the course of your work. Your ability to connect and your level of competence will dictate how you are perceived as a leader. Leaders at all levels need to increase their gravitational force by working on their connectivity and their competence.

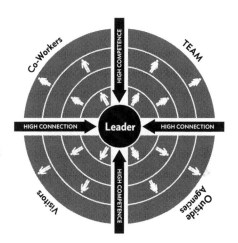

The title of Marshall Goldsmith's book has become a popular saying: "What got you here won't get you there" — but when it comes to leadership, that isn't true. Many companies promote people who are great in their current role instead of those who promise to be great at the next level. According to executive search firm Heidrick & Struggles, of those new senior level leaders, 40% fail in the first 18 months.[1] In most cases, these leaders are individuals who have

---

1   Kevin Kelly, CEO of Executive Search Firm, Heidrick & Struggles, https://www.primegenesis.com/our-blog/2009/04/40-percent-of-execs-pushed-out-fail-or-quit-within-18-months/.

demonstrated prior success and a high level of competence. If leaders at the highest level fail in such a short period of time, imagine the failure rate with less-experienced leaders.

Many companies promote people who are great in their current role instead of those who promise to be great at the next level.

Aspiring and existing leaders need a new saying, "What *got* me here won't *keep* me here." I know this because when I was a young leader managing five departments, I thought I was the best leader in the world. Why else would they give me so much responsibility? It wasn't until I initiated a leadership development program called Teleoemetrics[2] that I found out how wrong I was. To become the lead trainer for the program within my organization, I first attended a week-long train-the-trainer program. Before attending, I had to answer the same questions that I would be asking our leaders to answer during the in-house training. I also had to have my supervisor and subordinates answer those same questions as they related to their perception of my leadership.

During the train-the-trainer program, we had to open our packets — which contained feedback from our supervisors and subordinates — to see how our own perceptions of our leadership acumen compared to our supervisors' and subordinates' perceptions. It was in that humbling moment that I realized I wasn't a great leader after all and — to be honest with you — I'm still not a great leader. I am, however, the best kind of leader: a learning leader.

---

2   Teleometrics was the world's leading developer and publisher of scientifically validated training materials and personal feedback instruments for over 30 years.

"Learning Leaders"

Learning leaders do two things: they expand their knowledge and they seek feedback. First, they take the time to learn more about their current job and what that job looks like at the next level (e.g., if they're the supervisor of the Training Department and want to be the manager). They pursue knowledge outside of their area of expertise. They also seek to do more than just *learn* about leadership skills — they apply and adapt them. Second, they seek feedback from their subordinates and peers on a regular basis. The tricky part is soliciting criticism, especially from your direct reports. No one wants to be the one to tell their boss they made a mistake or could have handled a situation differently. And, truth be told, few of us have the courage to ask.

Learning leaders do two things: they expand their knowledge and they seek feedback.

If you've ever watched a TV show or movie that takes place in the military, you've probably heard the phrase "Permission to speak freely." If you want your subordinates and peers to give you honest feedback, you need to give them permission to speak freely. Most people aren't going to voluntarily tell you what you need to hear — especially if you have power over their future. So, if you want honest feedback, you're going to have to ask for it.

You need to give them a "get-out-of-jail-free card," but not just verbally. Give them a written guarantee that there will be no retribution — a guarantee that establishes the parameters for giving feedback. This may sound extreme but for some it will be necessary until they see that you are serious about receiving feedback. Be specific about the type and timing of the feedback you desire. Do you want them to share their opinions on training, how you treat people, how you conduct team meetings, or some other aspect of your leadership? When you ask specific questions and give them permission to speak freely, you'll get the answers you need to increase your LCS and your LCR (i.e., to be seen as a leader with the kind of confidence that has a gravitational pull and the kind of competence that makes others trust your abilities).

A leader who is well-regarded is the only kind of leader who can succeed. The truth is that, in the end, leaders don't do the work — they get the work done with and through other people. But you must first get those people to follow you by earning their respect and confidence. Just like you can't make a horse drink even if you lead it to water, you can't make your team follow you just because you have a fancy title, a bit of power, or a corner office. However, you *can* — with the right mindset — get them to gravitate toward you. Leaders at all levels need to increase their gravitational force by working on their connectivity and their competence. Now it's time to get your G-Force on.

Reflection Question for Lesson 27: Take time to seriously consider how you would rate both your LCS (Leadership Connectivity Score) and your LCR (Leadership Competency Rating) using a scale of 1 (Weak) to 10 (Strong). When evaluating your LCS, look at all those you interact with at work — not just your team members.

Time for a break! When you're ready, move ahead to another chapter/lesson and then come back to the following START Activity and Passport exercise during your second read-through of the book.

START Activity

―――――――

Increase Your G-Force

1. Make a list of ways you can expand your leadership knowledge. Consider:

    –   Your current position/job

    –   What you need to know to get to the next level

    –   Areas of interest outside your area of expertise

2. Seek feedback from peers and subordinates. Here's how to start:

    –   Define the specific types of feedback you want

    –   Choose a thoughtful cross-section of people to provide the feedback

    –   Ask them for their input and give them permission to speak freely

3. Look for ways to increase your G-Force with the other three groups (i.e., coworkers, visitors, and outside agencies) — not just your team.

4. Put the plan in motion.

Leadership Education & Application Passport

Part A – *Work with your leadership mentor to complete the Target Outcome and Actions sections below.*

Skill: Getting people to gravitate toward you.

Target Outcome: With whom will you be applying this skill and what are you hoping to accomplish?

_____

_____

_____

_____

Actions: What actions need to be taken before and during the application of this skill?

- _____

- _____

- _____

- _____

- _____

Part B – *Now, take a moment with your leadership mentor to review the results and explore what you took away from this experience of soliciting feedback and connecting in many circles. Look for ways to improve your ongoing experiences in this regard.*

Results:

* _____

* _____

* _____

* _____

* _____

Takeaways:

* _____

* _____

* _____

* _____

* _____

Once you have completed Parts A and B above, have your leadership mentor initial and date the stamp for this Lesson.

Congratulations! You are one step closer to being the leader you've always dreamed of being.

"Life is about not knowing, having to change, taking the moment and making the best of it, without knowing what's going to happen next."

— *Gilda Radner*

FACE It

Fast-Forwarding Through the Change Curve

"RUN!!" It was the last word I heard before being lifted off my feet while a knife was pressed into my neck. It was 10:00 p.m. on a hot summer Saturday night in El Paso, Texas. I was walking home from the 7-Eleven with a cherry Slurpee in my hand. I was with my friend Bimbo and we were doing what most 13-year-old boys do ... talking about girls. Four houses from where I lived on Mount Shasta, Bimbo yelled "RUN!!" and took off like a shot. I felt the razor-thin edge of the knife nick the side of my neck as I was pulled off my feet. Talk about a life-changing moment.

Two 18-year-old men said they were undercover cops. The one with the knife said, "We're looking for Rosa. She lives in this neighborhood."

I said, "I don't know anyone named Rosa."

He replied, "Well, you little *pendejo*, if you don't tell me where she is, I'm going to slit your throat."

I know what you are thinking — cops don't go around holding people at knifepoint. I knew that, but I wasn't going to argue the point. I just wanted to survive.

After what seemed like an eternity, I heard another word, "FREEZE!" When I looked up, I saw a wall of people holding shotguns. I'd never felt such an immediate sense of relief. All four of our parents quickly surrounded the two assailants and escorted them to my house at gunpoint.

You'd think that would be the end of the story. But just as the second guy was getting ready to step into our house, he shoved my mom into the wall and took off running. For some unexplainable reason, I took off after him. I chased him down the block to the next intersection, where he turned left onto Blue Ridge Drive. I finally caught up to him at the dead end, where I promptly jumped on his back and started choking him. I could hear the police sirens in the background getting closer. The closer they got, the harder he fought for his freedom. Suddenly, he fell backward, slamming me into the hard-packed gravel, leaving me stunned and gasping for air as he struggled to his feet. He ran down one side of the drainage ditch and up the other toward the park a quarter mile away. The cops eventually caught up with him; in the end, he and his buddy went to jail for assault with a deadly weapon and impersonating police officers.

Now, fast-forward two weeks. My mom comes to me and says, "Danny, I need you to go to the 7-Eleven and pick up a few personal items. I said, "Mom, I can't go ... I'm terrified of the dark." She said, "Danny, I understand — especially after what happened. But that was nothing compared to what I'm going to do to you if you don't go to the store." Perhaps you've heard the song by Jim Croce that says: "You don't tug on Superman's cape, you don't spit into the wind." Well, he left one out ... you don't say no to your red-headed, Irish mother when she's in a mood and she owns a shotgun.

I knew that if I was going to survive my trip to the store, I had to have a plan. But I couldn't figure out how to sneak out of the house with a shotgun. So I went to Plan B — I decided to ride my bike down the middle of the street as fast as I possibly could. As soon as I sat on my bike, I realized two things. First, the front tire was flat. Second, the back tire was flat. Then I thought, *"What am I going to do?"* You guessed it — I went straight to Plan C. I took off peddling as fast as I could down the middle of the street on my bike with two flat tires. I made it to the 7-Eleven and back ... safe and sound. Safe from the streets and safe from my mom.

Fast-Forwarding Through the Change Curve: The Five Lessons I Learned

We've all experienced change, but it's not the changes we choose to make that cause us difficulty. It's the changes that are imposed on us that cause our emotions to spike. When change happens to us, we are expected to be on board with the new vision. The problem is that our brains are lazy and prefer the status quo over change. And that problem is why my keynote, "Getting Comfortable with the Discomfort of Change," is so popular. That discomfort can stymie careers and handcuff organizations. If we're willing to examine the discomfort of change, there's so much we can learn.

Let's go back to that night I was held at knife point, difficult as it is to recall. That experience taught me five lessons that can help you FACE it and fast-forward through the emotions that change brings about. FACE is an acronym for the reactions we can experience during trauma or change: fear, anger, caution, or excitement. And fast-forwarding through change can position us for success — in our careers as well as in life.

Lesson 1: Let people know in advance about changes that will impact them. Bimbo let me know, but not soon enough. His "run!" came at the same time that I was grabbed by my assailant. When change is imposed (and thankfully most workplace change isn't as traumatic as being held at knife point), most people have one of four reactions: fear, anger, caution, or excitement (i.e., FACE reactions). If you let people know well in advance of the change, you can help them cope with their emotions before the change takes place. This will make implementing the change easier.

Lesson 2: Ask yourself and your team members: "Will this change kill me? If not, what is the worst thing that can happen? In the worst-case scenario, what are my options?"

Lesson 3: When you are confronted by change, assemble a team. The key is to select team members who can support you, help you facilitate the change, and — in some cases — help others accept the change and move forward or help them realize this may no longer be the right place for them. In my case, that team was a friend with fast feet and four parents armed with shotguns.

Lesson 4: Don't let a small win cause you to be overconfident in how the change is progressing. If you do, you may end up on your back gasping for air while the change runs out of control — like when I chased after the guy who got away.

Lesson 5: Most leaders fail to prepare *themselves* for change, let alone properly prepare their team members. You need a clear plan that motivates your team to take action in the right direction — in a fast and effective way. The key is your ability to adapt when the vision or plan does not go the way you anticipated, like when I rode my bike with two flat tires down the middle of the street.

Now, let's explore the four emotional responses to change: fear, anger, caution, or excitement (i.e., FACE).

Fear – When change is announced, there are many unanswered questions that flood the minds of your team members. One of the biggest areas of concern: "What does this mean for me? Will I still have a job? Will I have the same job or have to take a different job at a lower rate?" These fears can cause anxiety, stress, and even physical illness. Your job as a leader is to answer as many of those questions as you can up front and apply Lesson 2 by answering "of course not!" to the question, "Will it kill me?"

Anger – Some team members will react to change with hostility, resentment, and aggression. Their anger may result in an emotional outburst; they might leave the company so they can avoid the change altogether; and, in some cases, the anger people feel in the face of change can result in sabotage. Sabotage can be incredibly damaging to an organization. Angry people may attempt to create unrest within their social work groups through gossiping, backstabbing and false claims, which can sabotage change efforts. If ignored, this kind of negativity can spread. You must immediately let offenders know that their behavior is unacceptable and will not be tolerated. Recall my Lesson 3 from being mugged: assembling a team can help you mitigate the negative impact these people have. Make sure you include people who respond with enthusiasm on this team.

Caution – Not all team members will respond negatively to change. Some will approach change with caution, while they wait to see how the change will affect them personally. With the right support, these team members can become advocates for the change. To facilitate advocacy, you need to ensure every team member understands the need for change, you need to communicate regularly and you need to include them in the change process.

Excitement – There is also a group of people who embraces change and sees it as an opportunity. They know that for a company to survive, it must adapt to the changes in the marketplace. If you acknowledge their enthusiasm, this group can help you drive the change process. With your support and by delegating some of the change tasks, this group can positively influence the fearful, the angry, and the cautious.

In the end, we must be prepared to navigate change (and even crisis) at work and it's vital that we remember that actions speak louder than words. What you *do* is more important than what you *say*. When you treat people with dignity and respect throughout the cycle of change, you'll get the behavior you want from others. This means you must FACE it and apply the five lessons while referring frequently to your plan for implementing change. Be open and honest when responding to employee questions and concerns. When you do this, you'll be able to shorten the time it takes to achieve change and reduce the depth of the emotional response by your team members.

Reflection Question for Lesson 28: Think about the most recent change you've experienced and think about how it impacted you emotionally. Were you fearful, angry, cautious, enthusiastic, or all of the above? How did you handle it?

_____

_____

_____

_____

Time for a break! When you're ready, move ahead to another chapter/lesson and then come back to the following START Activity and Passport exercise during your second read-through of the book.

START Activity

_____

Help your team fast-forward through the change curve.

Big and small changes are almost a constant in business today. Apply the five lessons to your next workplace change and consider the four basic emotional reactions to change.

1. Let people know in advance about changes that will impact them.

2. Ask "Will this change kill me?"

3. Identify your team.

4. Celebrate achieving targets but don't get overly confident.

5. Be adaptable when things go sideways.

Leadership Education & Application Passport

Part A – *Work with your leadership mentor to complete the Target Outcome and Actions sections below.*

Skill: Fast-Forwarding Through the Change Curve

Target Outcome: With whom will you be applying this skill and what are you hoping to accomplish?

_____

_____

_____

_____

Actions: What actions need to be taken before and during the application of this skill?

- _____

- _____

- _____

- _____

- _____

Part B – *Now, take a moment with your leadership mentor to review the results and explore what you took away from this experience of helping your team through the change curve. Look for ways to improve your ongoing experiences in this regard.*

Results:

- _____
- _____
- _____
- _____
- _____

Takeaways:

- _____
- _____
- _____
- _____
- _____

Once you have completed Parts A and B above, have your leadership mentor initial and date the stamp for this Lesson.

Congratulations! You are one step closer to being the leader you've always dreamed of being.

"Those who plan do better than those who do not plan, even though they rarely stick to their plan."

— *Winston Churchill*

Row, Row, Row Your Boat

Keeping Your Project on Course

Think about a time when you had a great idea for a project or activity, whether it be at home or at work. Do you remember thinking, "This is going to be a piece of cake!"? That's exactly what I was thinking as I looked across Lake Cora in Paw Paw, Michigan, contemplating a sightseeing kayak trip around the lake. Standing on the bank, I saw that the water looked calm — smooth as glass. Who would have thought kayaking 2.5 miles around a lake would have presented any challenge? Certainly not me.

The first eighth of a mile with the slight breeze at my back was like gliding across silk. I was enjoying paddling through the morning mist rising up off the water while watching the Great Blue Heron fishing off the docks with their long legs and beaks. The remainder of my trip around the lake, however, was much more of a struggle than I anticipated, especially after such a smooth start. Once I came around the other side of the lake, the slight breeze was enough to create an unseen current pushing me in the opposite direction, making me work harder for every inch of progress.

Not only did the breeze cause me to stray off-course but my line of sight did, as well! If I turned to look at a house on the lake or the beautiful landscape, my kayak would go in that direction. I quickly learned that your boat goes where your eyes rove. To stay on course, I had to focus my attentions on stationary objects like the diving platforms and piers floating between the houses. This worked well until I got to a section of the lake where there were no houses. No houses meant no docks or diving platforms.

When you have a lot of open water in front of you, it's difficult to judge how far you have left to go and how fast you're traveling. I felt like I wasn't making any headway. Have you ever felt like you were working hard and getting nowhere? How did it make you feel? I felt discouraged. What does this have to do with leading a project or running a business? What can we learn from my trip around the lake? So much!

First, projects may be more difficult than they first appear. No matter how simple a project may seem, there will always be hidden currents that will try to force you off-course. There's a big difference between standing on shore and visualizing a nice smooth trip around the lake and actually getting into the water. Before beginning any project, let your team know that no matter how well they've plotted their course, there will always be unforeseen forces pushing against them.

No matter how simple a project may seem, there will always be hidden currents that will try to force you off-course.

I'm a big action-movie fan and one of my favorite movies is *Bad Boys II* with Will Smith and Martin Lawrence. In the movie, the main characters seek to rescue Marcus Burnett's sister from drug lords in Cuba. Once they get his sister, they are supposed to make their way to the escape tunnel but get cut off. Will Smith's character, Mike Lowery, radios the rest of the team and tells them, "We're going to Plan B." His partner Marcus says, "What's Plan B?" Plan "B" is supposed to take them directly to Guantanamo Bay U.S. Naval Base. Halfway to Guantanamo, they take a detour (Plan "C") through the drug shacks. The point is that you can make all the plans you want but things rarely go as planned.

To keep your projects on course, teach your people to SOAR.

Situation | Outcome | Actions | Record

Situation – Use the question "What if?" and have the team list situations that could potentially push them off-course during the project. Review previous projects to see what problems, delays, or glitches impacted the successful and timely achievement of the project. There are many ways a project can get off track; identifying potential risks is the first step to success.

Outcome – Next, look at each of the issues identified in the situation phase and define the possible outcomes for each.

Actions – Then decide what actions to take to get the project back on course using the If/Then method. Ask, "If this happens, then we can do, this, this, or this." Defining easily executable actions will go a long way in mitigating and resolving any situation before it gets out of control.

Record – Once your team has identified the potential situations, the possible outcomes for each and the actions available to you, record the information in a conspicuous place where the team gathers to discuss and work on the project. Having this information in a visible place will make it easier for the team to adapt to any situations that may come up.

Keep in mind that if your team's targets are too far apart, they can become discouraged and easily distracted by other tasks, projects, or assignments. By using the diving platforms as a checkpoint during my kayaking adventure, it was easy for me to stay focused while making my way around the lake, even though it was not going as I had hoped. The platforms were spaced far enough apart that they were achievable but not too far apart to cause me to become discouraged. As long as I had the platform in sight, I could see that I was making progress. When there were no platforms — just open water — I had no way to determine how fast I was going or if I was making any headway at all.

To keep yourself and your team motivated, reduce the space to stay on pace. What do I mean by that? It's simple. To be successful with any project, it's important to take time to anticipate potential setbacks, to work toward incremental targets, and stay focused on your goal. The SOAR method is a great way to help your team stay on track and maintain forward momentum. Here's to "Fair winds and following seas" for all your projects!

Pro Tip: The SOAR method can also be used on the fly to think through situations that happen in your routine tasks. Simply define the situation, take stock of the outcome, list possible courses of action, record the results and share them to prevent the situation from repeating in the future. You don't have to reserve the method only for big projects or initiatives — it works wherever you need it.

Reflection Question for Lesson 29: What was something that didn't go well today and how could you have used the SOAR method to expedite a positive outcome?

_____

_____

_____

_____

Time for a break! When you're ready, move ahead to another chapter/lesson and then come back to the following START Activity and Passport exercise during your second read-through of the book.

START Activity

___

Using the SOAR method to keep your projects on course.

1. Apply the SOAR method to your next project.

2. Create your action plan and include who will do what by when, where, and how.

3. Create multiple targets to support the overall goal. Remember to reduce the space between check-ins to stay on pace.

4. Ask "What if?" and have the team list situations that could potentially push them off-course

5. Identify the issues identified in the situation phase and define the possible outcomes for each.

6. Using if/then, determine actions you can take if the project gets off course.

7. Post potential outcomes and actions in a visible place.

Leadership Education & Application Passport

Part A – *Work with your leadership mentor to complete the Target Outcome and Actions sections below.*

Skill: Keeping Your Project on Course

Target Outcome: With whom will you be applying this skill and what are you hoping to accomplish?

_____

_____

_____

_____

Actions: What actions need to be taken before and during the application of this skill?

- _____
- _____
- _____
- _____
- _____

Part B – *Now, take a moment with your leadership mentor to review the results and explore what you took away from this experience of applying the "SOAR method" for keeping projects on course. Look for ways to improve your ongoing experiences in this regard.*

Results:

- _____
- _____
- _____
- _____
- _____

Takeaways:

- _____
- _____
- _____
- _____
- _____

Once you have completed Parts A and B above, have your leadership mentor initial and date the stamp for this Lesson.

Congratulations! You are one step closer to being the leader you've always dreamed of being.

"No story lives unless someone wants to listen.
The stories we love best do live in us forever."

— *J.K. Rowling*

The Bus Lady

Leadership Lessons
That Linger

In August 2012, I competed in the semi-finals of the World Championship of Public Speaking in Orlando. The competition starts with 30,000 contestants and culminates in the crowning of a single winner. I took first place through the first four of six levels of competition, making me one of just 86 people to make it to the semi-finals.

By the end of the semi-finals, as we say here in Kentucky, I didn't win, place, or show. I couldn't believe I didn't make it to the finals. I was upset and I told my wife I wasn't attending the rest of the conference. Instead, we spent the day at Disney World. It was a great day! At 10:30 that night, sitting on the bus headed back to our room at the conference center, I learned one of my most valuable lessons of my life.

My wife and I were sitting three rows back on the passenger side. I was wearing cargo shorts, a t-shirt, Indiana Jones-style hat, and sunglasses. Yes, sunglasses — at night. I thought I was being cool, I guess. A lady sitting in the seat just behind the driver turned to me and said, "I heard your speech yesterday. I needed to hear your life-changing message. Thank you for sharing it!"

The power of her words didn't really sink in until the next day, upon further reflection about that chance moment. You see, this lady, the Bus Lady as I have come to affectionately call her, had only seen me one other time in her life — when I was standing on a stage in a suit and tie. Yet, my message had created such an impact in her life that, when she saw me on the bus, she was able to see through my "disguise." That's when it hit me — we all have stories and, through the power of storytelling, we have the ability to change lives.

Listening to a great story is like riding a rollercoaster. Think of the emotional highs and lows you experience when you watch a movie. It's the ups and downs that engage our emotions. One of my speaking mentors, Patricia Fripp, says, "There are two ways to connect to your audience, intellectually and emotionally. You don't *have* to connect emotionally — unless you want your ideas to be remembered." Therefore, it's critical for leaders to be intentional about the stories they tell.

It's critical for leaders to be intentional about the stories they tell.

As a leader, it is critical that you influence your team members (their behaviors and their attitudes) and the only way to do this is to first connect with them. So, it stands to reason that you should be able to tell compelling stories to your team members, boss, other department heads, customers, and anyone else you need to influence. Leaders who are able to tell great stories have the power to persuade. However, a great story told poorly doesn't have that same power. Have you ever listened to someone tell a story that wandered here and there with no discernable point? When a story lacks structure it also lacks power.

Certified World Class Speaking Coaches use a structure we call the "Skeletal Story" to outline the stories we tell. It consists of 5 C's — Characters, Conflict, Cure, Change, and Carryout Message. It's a method that works as well at work as it does on stage — and work is where the stakes are often highest.

Characters

Figure out who the main characters are in your story with brief descriptions (physical and emotional). If there are more than three, try to combine the actions of the characters down to two or three — otherwise it could get confusing for the audience.

Conflict

A story without conflict is like the difference between eating a rice cake or a box of freshly popped popcorn covered in butter. One is boring and bland while the other makes your mouth water and your hand go back for more. Imagine the *Rocky* fight scene with Rocky and Apollo Creed circling each other for 15 rounds, neither ever throwing a punch. Without a well-defined conflict, your audience will be just as bored. The more the conflict intensifies, the more your audience will be engaged.

Cure/Climax

The cure is the tipping point in the story. It gives your audience the perfect return on their time investment. It's the moment they've been waiting for — the reason they have been sitting on the edge of their seats.

Change

If there is no change in one of the characters, there is no story. The whole point of storytelling in leadership is to illustrate a change in behavior that can be held up as an example of what to do or not to do.

Carryout Message

Your carryout message should motivate your audience to take action. To that end, ask yourself, "What is it I want my audience to know, think, do, or feel at the end?" Your carryout message should be no more than 10 words, and ideally around five to seven. It should also be rhythmic in nature. I've often heard storytelling expert Craig Valentine say it should be so simple a five-year-old can repeat it.

The idea is to capture the essence of the 5 C's in five sentences:

1. *Characters* – I competed against 30,000 contestants in the World Championship of Public Speaking.

2. *Conflict* – I felt like a failure because I didn't win.

3. *Cure* – The Bus Lady said, "Your story changed my life."

4. *Change* – I learned that it's not about winning trophies; it's about winning hearts.

5. *Carryout Message* – Share a Story, Change a Life.

Let It Flow

There are many types of storytelling "flows" — some more convoluted than others. Because most leadership lessons need to be conveyed quickly, I suggest the "Dive-In" or the "Set-Up" flows.

Dive-In – The storyteller dives right into the conflict. If you have too much pre-ramble (i.e., too long of an introduction and ramp-up), you run the risk of your audience tuning out.

Set-Up – There will be instances when you can highlight positive elements about the character before plunging him deep into conflict. This makes the conflict more intense. In my story, the Set-Up before the conflict is when I tell you I competed with 30,000 contestants and took first place in the first four of six levels of competition, making me one of 86 people to make it to the semi-finals. Then I share that after giving my semi-final speech, I didn't win, place, or show. Remember, the further the fall, the deeper the connection. Oh! That sounds a lot like a carryout message.

When you master these basic storytelling components, you will be better able to move people emotionally. It will make it easier for you to influence others to buy your product, increase productivity, change habits, and buy into your vision.

Reflection Question for Lesson 30: What are some of your favorite stories to tell and what lesson, if any, do they deliver?

_____

_____

_____

_____

Time for a break! When you're ready, move ahead to another chapter/lesson and then come back to the following START Activity and Passport exercise during your second read-through of the book.

START Activity

**Create a Skeletal Story outline using the 5 C's
— a story that you will ultimately use to convey
a lesson to a subordinate or coworker.**

Characters:

_____

_____

Conflict:

_____

_____

Cure:

_____

_____

Change:

_____

_____

Carryout Message:

_____

_____

Leadership Education & Application Passport

Part A – *Work with your leadership mentor to complete the Target Outcome and Actions sections below.*

Skill: Sharing Leadership Lessons That Linger

Target Outcome: With whom will you be applying this skill and what are you hoping to accomplish?

_____

_____

_____

_____

Actions: What actions need to be taken before and during the application of this skill?

- _____

- _____

- _____

- _____

- _____

Part B – *Now, take a moment with your leadership mentor to review the results and explore what you took away from this experience of crafting leadership stories using the 5 C's and a strategic story flow. Look for ways to improve your ongoing experiences in this regard.*

Results:

- _____
- _____
- _____
- _____
- _____

Takeaways:

- _____
- _____
- _____
- _____
- _____

Once you have completed Parts A and B above, have your leadership mentor initial and date the stamp for this Lesson.

Congratulations! You are one step closer to being the leader you've always dreamed of being.

"Procrastination is the bad habit of putting off until the day after tomorrow what should have been done the day before yesterday."

— *Napoleon Hill*

Free Crab Tomorrow

Stop Procrastinating

You've probably attended a professional training program and thought, "I really enjoyed the content and I picked up some really good ideas." Then you left the training, went about your normal day, went to bed, and promptly forgot all about the great content that you had every intention of putting to use. Unfortunately, unless you apply new information fairly quickly, it simply fades away — resulting in a waste of *your time* and the *company's money*. Almost half of the $70 billion spent on employee training in the United States falls in the category of scrap training — training that is delivered but never applied on the job.

I remember the first time I ate at a Joe's Crab Shack restaurant. I was sitting in a booth when I turned and saw one of those table tents that read, "Free Crab Tomorrow." For about half a second, I was ready to leave the restaurant and come back the next day — that is until I realized it was just a marketing ploy. If you've ever seen the *Rocky* movies, you'll remember the scene where Apollo Creed is training

Rocky for his rematch with Clubber Lang. In the scene, Apollo is pounding Rocky ... and Rocky isn't fighting back. Finally, Apollo says, "Damn Rocky, what's the matter with you?" Rocky says, "Tomorrow." Then Apollo says, "There is no tomorrow, there is no tomorrow, there is no tomorrow."

It doesn't matter if you want to exercise more, lose weight, get organized, or stop smoking, most of us have been guilty of saying, "Tomorrow." Why is tomorrow so much more appealing than today? Because if we put off everything to tomorrow, we don't have to deal with it today — we don't have to face our fears, we don't have to put in the hard work, and we get to stay in our comfort zone where we feel safe.

Why is tomorrow so much more appealing than today?

I recently had a run-in with the lure of "tomorrow." I'm no Rocky, but I wanted to start going back to the gym. I reasoned that there wasn't time. You see, I was in the middle of writing a book and didn't want to take 90 minutes out of my day to drive to the gym, workout for an hour, and drive back home. But the truth is, that is just an excuse. There will always be a reason why we can't do something.

So, what do you do to get past the excuses? I suggest five simple tips. First, be clear about what you want to accomplish. Second, make a list of actions you need to take to achieve what you want. Third, make a list of all the reasons (i.e., excuses) that are keeping you from acting today. Fourth, think of ways to get around those reasons (i.e., excuses) and take one small step today. Fifth, take one new step each day until you've achieved what you were hoping to accomplish.

My excuses for not getting back into a workout habit were twofold: I didn't want to take 90 minutes out of my writing day to work out and

I didn't want to look like a weakling when I went back to the gym. At the beginning of my writing journey for this book, I got in the habit of stopping every hour for five minutes to stretch and get a drink of water. So, I decided to take that five minutes every hour and do push-ups and sit-ups before getting a drink. By the time I finish this book, my goal is to be able to do 100 push-ups without stopping. This way I don't have to take time away from writing, I increase my fitness and when I go back to the gym I won't be as self-conscious about how much weight I can initially lift.

The tendency to procrastinate strikes at work just as often as it strikes in our personal lives. When it comes to your personal leadership development or the development of your leaders, it's easier to say "Tomorrow" than it is to take that first step today. Every day you put off your leadership development is another missed opportunity for you to make a difference as a leader. The most difficult thing for most people who want to make a change or develop a skill is taking that first step. The good news is that, by reading this book, you've taken that first step — and if you've read all 31 lessons, you've taken several steps ... all in the right direction.

Reflection Question for Lesson 31: What is something you really want to pursue or achieve but have been putting off? What are your reasons for putting it off?

_____

_____

_____

_____

Time for a break! When you're ready, move ahead to another chapter/lesson and then come back to the following START Activity and Passport exercise during your second read-through of the book.

START Activity

Stop procrastinating by tackling what's getting in your way.

What is the one thing you really want but have been putting off for various reasons?

- First, be clear about what you want to accomplish.

- Second, make a list of actions you need to take to achieve what you want.

- Third, make a list of all the reasons (i.e., excuses) that are keeping you from acting today.

- Fourth, think of ways to get around those reasons (i.e., excuses) and take one small step today.

- Fifth, take one new step each day until you achieve what you were hoping to accomplish.

Leadership Education & Application Passport

Part A – *Work with your leadership mentor to complete the Target Outcome and Actions sections below.*

Skill: Overcoming Procrastination

Target Outcome: With whom will you be applying this skill and what are you hoping to accomplish?

_____

_____

_____

_____

Actions: What actions need to be taken before and during the application of this skill?

- _____
- _____
- _____
- _____
- _____

Part B – *Now, take a moment with your leadership mentor to review the results and explore what you took away from this experience of tackling procrastination with five simple steps. Look for ways to improve your ongoing experiences in this regard.*

Results:

* _____

* _____

* _____

* _____

* _____

Takeaways:

* _____

* _____

* _____

* _____

* _____

Once you have completed Parts A and B above, have your leadership mentor initial and date the stamp for this Lesson.

Congratulations! You are one step closer to being the leader you've always dreamed of being.

Conclusion

Information is only a collection of ideas that are spoken, written, read, seen, and heard; knowledge happens when you can make sense of those ideas.

Information is only a collection of ideas that are spoken, written, read, seen and heard; knowledge happens when you can make sense of those ideas.

In *The Language of Leadership*, you have been provided with 31 standalone lessons. In order to transform the information contained in this book into *knowledge*, you must provide context. Context is the setting in which the information can be fully understood and assessed. Without context, information is meaningless. Take the following five letters — CLOSE. Without context, you have no idea if I am asking you to do something (close rather than open) or if I am indicating distance (close rather than far away). The same is true if you want to make sense of the information in this book. You must be willing to apply it in your setting, in your environment, in your workplace. Only then will it become knowledge. And applied knowledge drives results.

Becoming a great leader is not easy. I've had casual observers note that the skills I teach — in my books, my workshops and keynotes, and through my coaching — are "soft skills" (their words, not mine).

And I'll tell you what I say to that assessment: "If leadership is such a *soft* skill, why do so many people suck at it?" The vast majority of leaders, regardless of their deep expertise and broad experiences, have a difficult time applying the concepts vital to effective leadership. Mastering the *soft* skills takes *hard* work. Indeed, leadership is not for the faint of heart — it takes courage. Without leadership, we would still be wearing loin cloths and cowering in a cave while the saber-toothed tiger anxiously awaited its next meal. It took someone with courage and the ability to motivate the rest of the clan to take up arms to slay the tiger.

The good news is that you're not being asked to slay a saber-toothed tiger — just to have the courage to be vulnerable enough to take the information in this book and apply it. Of course, you won't get the satisfaction of eating a nice rack of fall-off-the-bone saber-toothed tiger short ribs. You, my friend, will get something far more satisfying and rewarding — you'll get that warm feeling deep inside that lasts a lifetime and comes from watching someone you've led become all you believed they could ... watching them learn, grow, and improve.

Have the courage to be vulnerable enough to take the information in this book and apply it.

Epilogue

As this book ends and the credits roll by, you will find me sitting beneath my gazebo — gazing at the beauty that surrounds me and thinking about the chaotic state of the world just beyond my oasis. As this book heads to its readers, it's the summer of 2020 and change is happening in every conceivable way. We are in the midst of a global pandemic, global social unrest, and global political unrest — all the result of a chronic and widespread decayed sense of leadership.

We live in a time when workplace leaders lack the ability to engage and inspire their employees; when local civic leaders fail to take action to stifle violence or protect public health or support the economic livelihoods of the people they're charged to serve; and countries poke and prod each other to see how far they can go before war breaks out.

Unlike the movies, there is no Captain Marvel or Superman to save us from the self-absorbed leadership of our day. There is only you.

And I need you. Your team members need you. Your community needs you. The world needs you!

Acknowledgments

Big thanks to:

First and foremost, my amazing wife, Mart. What can I say? You are the main reason I was able to take the time to write this book. I am so thankful that I have you in my corner, supporting me all the way. I look forward to sharing all the good that comes from this book with you! You are my bud and my hero! Thanks for not just believing, but *knowing*, that I could do this! I love you always and forever!

And to Silver Tree Publishing, especially my task master and meticulous editor, Kate Colbert, for giving my words the smooth finish of a fine bourbon (hey, I'm a writer and I live in Kentucky —what did you expect?) ... all while protecting my fragile writer's ego. You have an uncanny ability to refine a book's structure and find the right words to increase clarity while maintaining my voice at every turn. And to Courtney Hudson, for putting up with me and taking my vision and turning it into a visually engaging cover and interior layout. You have the patience of a saint!

And finally, to my clients, readers, friends, and family for their support and encouragement. You make it worth it. Day after day and page after page.

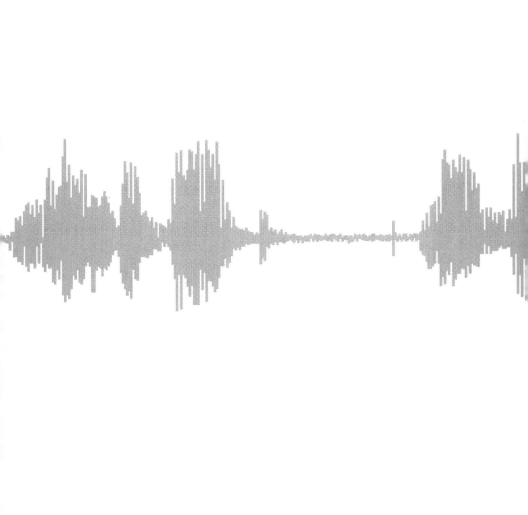

Keep in Touch!

To learn more about the programs Daniel offers, visit:

🌐　DanielDMatthews.com

To connect with Daniel and to see more great content and videos:

in　LinkedIn.com/in/DanDMatt

🐦　Twitter.com/DanDMatthews

▶　"Daniel D. Matthews" on YouTube

Send an email:

✉　dan@continue2improve.com

To order books in bulk and learn about volume discounts:

Send an email! Interested in ordering 25 or more copies of *The Language of Leadership* for your organization, association, or conference? Inquire at dan@continue2improve.com.

Go Beyond the Book

Learn more about *The Language of Leadership*, and pick up support materials and worksheets for the book at:

 NicerBarkNoBite.com

Hire Daniel to:

- Facilitate a Leadership Book Club to guide your leaders' journey through *The Language of Leadership*

- Provide individual and small group leadership coaching for your next generation of leaders

- Deliver a keynote, workshop or seminar on the principles of *The Language of Leadership*

- Develop other programs to help you lead, grow and improve your team

Get the conversation started at 859-699-5993 or dan@continue2improve.com.

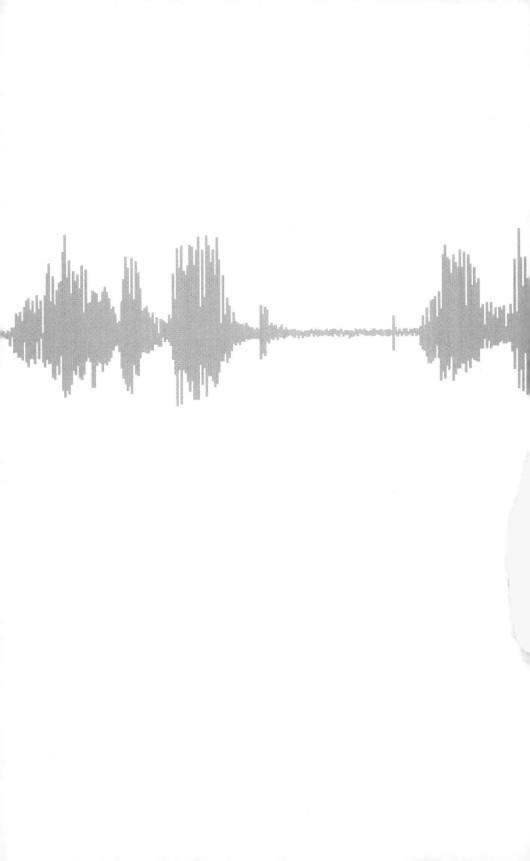

About the Author

Daniel D. Matthews is an accomplished leadership coach, problem-solving and change leadership expert, and speaker, best known for his ability to help leaders Step Up, Stand Out and Inspire Others. He is the Chief Continuous Improvement Officer of Continue 2 Improve, founded in 2011 on the heels of his acclaimed book, *The A3 Workbook: Unlock Your Problem-Solving Mind.* Daniel has been honored to train and 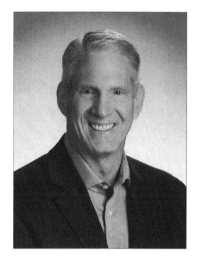 coach leaders through personal and institutional transformations — in small to medium-sized companies and within large globally recognized brands. His passion lies in helping leaders learn, grow and improve their teams.

Prior to starting his career as a speaker and consultant, Daniel was an integral part of Toyota's organizational development team, whose leadership programs have been taught all around the world. He coaches individuals to achieve their own version of the finish line, helping clients accomplish their business and revenue goals by providing them with the leadership training and tools needed to develop teams that start, finish and sustain meaningful improvements.

Daniel is originally from the mean streets of El Paso, Texas, but that's a story for another time and the subject of another book on SPEAR-heading Change. He now lives in Lexington, Kentucky, the horse capital of the world, with his wife and more Bonsai trees than she cares to water.

Wait! There's more ...

Most people don't know that Daniel is a great baker and an excellent cake decorator. He also loves the challenge of transforming a mish-mash of items from the refrigerator into savory, delicious dishes, which his wife refers to as Leftover Surprise.

Daniel is also an adrenaline junkie. He'll try almost anything once — from triathlons, to riding bulls, to jumping out of airplanes, to being electrocuted during Tough Mudders, and lots more in between. If he ever tires of traveling to serve his clients, he will work fulltime on his side hustle — training dogs.